how to develop a super-power memory

Harry Lorayne

how to
develop a
super-power
memory

Pan Books
London and Sydney

First published 1958 by A. Thomas and Company
Revised edition published 1963
This edition published 1977 by Pan Books Ltd,
Cavaye Place, London SW10 9PG
© Harry Lorayne 1958, 1963
ISBN 0 330 25104 X
Printed and bound in Great Britain by
Richard Clay (The Chaucer Press) Ltd, Bungay, Suffolk

Contents

Foreword

Mark Twain is reported to have said that 'everyone talks about the weather, but no one does anything about it'. Similarly, everyone talks or brags about their bad memory, but few people ever do anything about it. Let's face it, there isn't much you can do about the weather, but there's a great deal that you can do about your bad memory.

Many people have told me that they would 'give a million pounds' if they could acquire a memory like mine. Well, don't misunderstand me, I wouldn't turn down your offer of a million pounds; but actually the price of this book is all you need to spend.

This isn't true in its strictest sense; you'll also have to spend just a little bit of your time, and just a little effort to get the brain working. Once you've started on my system, you may be surprised as to how simple and obvious it really is.

If you purchased this book expecting a theoretical harangue of technical terms, you are doomed to disappointment. I have tried to write and explain the system as if I were sitting in your living-room and explaining it to you there.

Although, naturally, quite a bit of research was necessary, I've discarded most of the technical ideas and thoughts because I found them difficult to understand and to apply myself. I am an entertainer and a memory expert, not a psychiatrist or a doctor, and I didn't think it necessary to go into an explanation of the workings of the human brain, and just how the memory actually works in terms of cells, curves, impressions, etc.

So you will find that all the ways and methods in the

book are those that I use myself and therefore feel qualified to teach to you.

Psychologists and educationalists have said that we use only a small percentage of our brain power – I think the system here will enable you to use just a little more than average. So, if like your operations, you have been bragging about your poor memory, I think that after you've read this book you'll still brag about your memory, but to the other extreme. Now, you'll be able to boast of possessing a wonderfully retentive and accurate memory!

1 How keen is your observation?

Which light is on the top of the traffic light? Is it the *Red* or the *Green*? Your first thought, probably, is that this is an easy question to answer. However, put yourself in this position – you are on one of the current quiz shows that pays a lot of money for correct answers. You must answer this question correctly to win the top prize. Now then, which light is on top, the *Red* or the *Green*?

If you have been able to picture yourself in the above position, you are probably hesitating now, because you're not really sure which light is on top, are you? If you are sure, then you're one of the minority who has *observed* what most people only *see*. There is a world of difference between seeing and observing; proven, of course, by the fact that most of the people to whom I put the above question either give the wrong answer or are not sure. This, even though they see the traffic lights countless times every day!

By the way, *Red* is always on top of the traffic light, *Green* is always on the bottom. If there is a third colour, it is usually *Amber*, for caution, and that one is always in the centre. If you were sure that *Red* was the correct answer, let me see if I can't puncture your pride a bit with another observation test.

Don't look at your wrist watch! Don't look at your wrist watch, and answer this question: Is the number *six* on your watch dial the Arabic figure 6, or is it the Roman numeral VI? Think this over for a moment before you look at your watch. Decide on your answer as if it were really important that you answer correctly. You're on that quiz show again, and there's a lot of money at stake.

All right, have you decided on your answer? Now, look

at your watch and see if you were right. Were you? Or were you wrong in either case, because your watch doesn't have a *six* at all! The small dial that ticks off the seconds usually occupies that space on most modern watches.

Did you answer this question correctly? Whether you did or did not, you had to look at your watch to check. Can you tell now the *exact* time on your watch? Probably not, and you just looked at it a second ago! Again, you saw, but you didn't observe.

Try this on your friends. Although people see their watches innumerable times every day, few of them can tell you about the number *six*.

Don't feel too badly if you couldn't answer any of these questions; as I said before, most people can't. You may recall a film a few years ago which starred Ronald Colman, Celeste Holm and Art Linkletter. The picture was *Champagne for Caesar*, and it was about a man who couldn't be stumped with any question on a quiz show. The finale of the film was the last question of the quiz, which was worth some millions of pounds. To earn these millions, Ronald Colman was asked to give his own social security number. Of course, he didn't know it! This was amusing and interesting, to me, anyway, since it struck home. It proves, doesn't it, that people see but do not observe? Incidentally, do you know *your* National Health number?

Although the systems and methods contained in this book *make* you observe *automatically*, you will find some interesting observation exercises in a later chapter. The system will also make you use your imagination with more facility than ever before.

I've taken the time and space to talk about observation because it is one of the things important to training your memory. The other, and more important thing, is *association*. We cannot possibly remember anything that we do not observe. After something is observed, either by sight or hearing, it must, in order to be remembered, be associated in our minds with, or to, something we *already* know or remember.

Since you will observe automatically when using my system, it is association with which we will mostly concern ourselves.

Association, as pertaining to memory, simply means the connecting or tying up of two (or more) things to each other. Anything you manage to remember, or have managed to remember, is only due to the fact that you have subconsciously associated it to something else.

'Every Good Boy Does Fine.' – Does that sentence mean anything to you? If it does, then you must have studied music as a youngster. Almost every child that studies music is taught to remember the lines of the music staff or treble clef by remembering, 'Every Good Boy Does Fine'.

I've already stressed the importance of association, and I want to prove to you that you have used definite *conscious* associations many times before, without even realizing it. The letters E, G, B, D and F don't mean a thing. They are just letters, and difficult to remember. The sentence 'Every Good Boy Does Fine' does have meaning and is something you know and understand. The new thing, the thing you had to commit to memory, was associated with something you *already knew*.

The spaces of the music staff were committed to memory with the same system; the initial system. If you remembered the word 'face', you remembered that the spaces on the staff are F, A, C, and E. Again you associated something new and meaningless to something you already knew and to something that *had* meaning to you.

It is probably many years since you learned the jinglet, 'Thirty days hath September, April, June and November, all the rest have thirty-one', etc., but how many times have you relied on it when it was necessary to know the number of days in a particular month?

I am sure that many times you have seen or heard something which made you snap your fingers and say, 'Oh, that reminds me . . .' You were made to remember something by the thing you saw or heard, which usually had no obvious connection to the thing you remembered.

However, in your mind the two things were associated in some way. This was a subconscious association. Right now, I am pointing out a few examples of conscious associations at work; and they certainly do work. People who have forgotten many things that they learned in their early grades at school still remember the spaces and lines of the treble clef. If you have read this chapter so far, concentrating as you read, you should know them by now, even if you've never studied music.

One of the best examples I know is the one which was a great help to me in my early spelling classes. We were being taught that the word 'believe' was spelt with the e following the i. In order to help us to commit this to memory we were told to remember a short sentence, 'Never be*lie*ve a *lie*.'

This is a perfect instance of a conscious association. I know for a fact that many adults still have trouble spelling 'believe'. They are never quite sure if the i is first, or if it is the e. The spelling of the word 'believe' was the new thing to remember. The word 'lie' is a word we all *already* knew how to spell. None of the students that heard that little sentence ever again misspelled the word 'believe'. Do you have trouble spelling the word 'piece'? If you do, just remember the phrase '*pie*ce of *pie*'. This phrase will always tell you how to spell 'piece'.

Can you draw anything that resembles the map of England, from memory? How about China, Japan or Czechoslovakia? You probably can't draw any of these. If I had mentioned Italy, ninety per cent of you would have immediately seen a picture of a *boot* in your mind's eye. Is that right? If you did, and if you draw a boot, you will have the approximate outline of the map of Italy.

Why did this picture appear in your mind's eye? Only because, at one time or another, perhaps many years ago, you either heard or noticed that the map of Italy resembled a boot. The shape of Italy, of course, was the new thing to remember; the boot was the something we already knew and remembered.

You can see that simple conscious associations helped you memorize abstract information like the above examples very easily. The initial system that I mentioned earlier can be used to help you memorize many things. For example, if you wanted to remember the names of the Dionne quintuplets, you could try to remember the word 'macey'. This would help you to recall that the girls' names are Marie, Annette, Cecile, Emilie and Yvonne.

There's only one thing wrong with this idea in its present stage. There is nothing to make you remember that the word 'macey' is connected with the Dionne quintuplets, or vice versa.

If you remembered the word, fine, then you would probably know the names of the quins; but how do you remember the word? I'll show you how to do this in future chapters.

The systems and methods in this book will show you how the principles and ideas of simple conscious associations can be applied to remembering anything. Yes, that's right – remembering *anything*, including names and faces, items, objects, facts, figures, speeches, etc. In other words, the systems and methods you will learn in this book can be applied to anything and everything in everyday social or business life.

2 Habit is memory

I feel assured that there is no such thing as ultimate forgetting; traces once impressed upon the memory are indestructible.
Thomas de Quincey

An accurate and retentive memory is the basis of all business success. In the last analysis, *all* our knowledge is based on our memories. Plato said it this way, 'All knowledge is but remembrance'; while Cicero said of memory, it is 'the treasury and guardian of all things'. One strong example should suffice for the time being – you could not be reading this book right now if you didn't remember the sounds of the twenty-six letters of our alphabet!

This may seem a bit far-fetched to you, but it is true, nevertheless. Actually, if you were to lose your memory completely, you would have to start learning *everything* from scratch, just like a new-born baby. You wouldn't remember how to dress, or shave, or apply your make-up, or how to drive your car, or whether to use a knife or fork, etc. You see, all the things we attribute to habit should be attributed to memory. Habit *is* memory.

Mnemonics, which is a large part of a trained memory, is not a new or strange thing. As a matter of fact, the word 'mnemonic' is derived from the name of the Greek Goddess Mnemosyne; and memory systems were used as far back as early Greek civilization. The *strange* thing is that trained memory systems are not known and used by many more people. Most of those who *have* learned the secret of mnemonics in memory have been amazed, not only at their own tremendous ability to remember, but also at the kudos they received from their families and friends.

Some of them decided it was too good a thing to teach to

anyone else. Why not be the only man at the office who could remember every pattern number and price; why not be the only one who could get up at a party and demonstrate something that everyone marvelled at?

I, on the other hand, feel that trained memories should be brought to the foreground, and to this end this book is dedicated. Although some of you may know me as an entertainer, it is not my purpose, of course, to teach you a memory act. I have no desire to put you on the stage. I *do* want to teach you the wonderful practical uses of a trained memory. There are many memory stunts taught in this book; these are fine for showing your friends how bright you are. More important, they are excellent memory exercises, and the ideas used in all the stunts can be applied practically.

The question that people ask me most often is, 'Isn't it confusing to remember too much?' My answer to that is, 'No!' There is *no limit* to the capacity of the memory. Lucius Scipio was able to remember the names of all the people of Rome; Cyrus was able to call every soldier in his army by name; while Seneca could memorize and repeat two thousand words, after hearing them once.

I believe that the more you remember, the more you *can* remember. The memory, in many ways, is like a muscle. A muscle must be exercised and developed in order to give proper service and use; so must the memory. The difference is that a muscle can be overtrained or become musclebound while the memory cannot. You can be taught to have a trained memory just as you can be taught anything else. As a matter of fact, it is much easier to attain a trained memory than, say, to learn to play a musical instrument. If you can read and write English, and have a normal amount of common sense, *and* if you read and study this book, you will have acquired a trained memory! Along with the trained memory you will probably acquire a greater power of concentration, a purer sense of observation, and perhaps, a stronger imagination.

Remember, please, that *there is no such thing as a bad memory*! This may come as a shock to those of you who have used your supposedly 'bad' memories as an excuse for years. But, I repeat, there is no such thing as a bad memory. There are only trained or untrained memories. Almost all untrained memories are one-sided. That is to say that people who can remember names and faces cannot remember telephone numbers, and those who remember phone numbers can't, for the life of them, remember the names of the people they wish to call.

There are those who have a pretty good retentive memory, but a painfully slow one; just as there are some who can remember things quickly, but cannot retain them for any length of time. If you apply the systems and methods taught in this book, I can assure you a quick *and* retentive memory for just about anything.

As I mentioned in the previous chapter, anything you wish to remember must in some way or other be associated in your mind to something you already know or remember. Of course, most of you will say that you have remembered, or do remember, many things, and that you do not associate them with anything else. Very true! If you *were* associating *knowingly*, then you would already have the beginnings of a trained memory.

You see, most of the things you have ever remembered have been associated *subconsciously* with something else that you already knew or remembered. The important word here is 'subconsciously'. You yourselves do not realize what is going on in your subconscious; most of us would be frightened if we did. What you subconsciously associated strongly will be remembered, what was not associated strongly will be forgotten. Since this tiny mental callisthenic takes place without your knowledge, you cannot help it any.

Here then is the crux of the matter – I am going to teach you to associate anything you want to, *consciously*! When you have learned to do that, you will have acquired a trained memory!

Keep in mind that the system that I teach in this book is an *aid* to your normal or true memory. It is your true memory that does the work for you, whether you realize it

or not. There is a very thin line between a trained memory
and the true memory, and as you continue to use the system
taught here, that line will begin to fade.

That is the wonderful part about the whole thing; after
using my system consciously for a while it becomes
automatic and you almost start doing it subconsciously!

3 Test your memory

Some university students were taking an examination just prior to their Christmas vacation. This was an exam they hadn't looked forward to, since they knew it would be a difficult one. It was! One student handed in his paper with this remark on it: 'God only knows the answers to these questions. Merry Christmas!' The professor marked the papers, and returned them to the students. One had a message on it: 'God gets an A, you get an F. Happy New Year!'

I don't think you'll find the tests in this chapter quite as difficult. Even if you do, it doesn't matter, since no one will know how badly you do on them. In a previous chapter, I gave you a few examples showing how conscious associations are a great help in remembering anything. Such a simple aid to our memories, and yet so effective. The fact that those of you who learned the phrase 'Never believe a lie' never misspelled the word 'believe' again, proves their effectiveness. The more important fact that you can retain these simple associations over a period of years proves it still more.

It is my contention that if you can remember or retain one thing with the aid of a conscious association, you can do it with anything else. That's my contention and I intend to prove it *with you*; I also intend to prove it *to* you. After you've learned the methods, I'm sure you'll agree that conscious associations will be more useful and valuable to you than you ever imagined they could be. If I were to tell you now that after reading and studying the system in this book, you would be able to remember as high as a fifty-digit number, and *retain* it for as long as you liked, after looking at it only once – you would think me mad.

If I told you that you could memorize the order of a shuffled pack of fifty-two playing cards after hearing them called only once, you would think me mad! If I told you that you would never again be troubled by forgetting names or faces, or that you would be able to remember a shopping list of fifty items, or memorize the contents of an entire magazine, or remember prices and important telephone numbers, or know the day of the week of any date – you would surely think I had 'flipped my lid'. But read and study this book and see for yourself!

I imagine that the best way for me to prove it to you is to let you see your own progress. In order to do that, I must show you first how poor your untrained memory is. So take a few moments, right now, and mark yourselves on the tests that follow. In this way you will be able to take the same tests after reading certain chapters, and compare your scores.

I feel that these tests are quite important. Since your memory will improve with almost every chapter you read, I want you to *see* that improvement. That will give you confidence, which in itself is important to a trained memory. After each test you will find a space for your present score, and a space which is to be used for your score after reading those particular chapters.

One important point, before you take the tests – don't skip through the book and read only the chapters that you think will help you. *All* the chapters will help you, and it is much better if you read from one to the other. *Do not jump ahead*, of me, or yourself!

Test 1

Read this list of fifteen objects just once – you can take about two minutes to do so. Then try to write them, without looking at the book, of course, in exactly the same order in which they appear here. When scoring yourself, remember that if you leave out a word, that will make the remaining words incorrect, for they will be out of sequence. I will remind you to take this test again, after you've read Chapter 5. Give yourself 5 points for each correct one.

book, ashtray, cow, coat, match, razor, apple, purse, venetian blind, frying pan, clock, eyeglasses, door knob, bottle, worm.

Write your score here __ Score after learning Chapter 5 ___

Test 2

Take about three minutes to try to memorize the twenty objects listed here, by number. Then try to list them yourself without looking at the book. You must remember not only the object, but to which number it belongs. You'll be reminded to take this test again, after you've read Chapter 6. Give yourself 5 points for every object that you put with the correct number.

1. radio	6. telephone	11. dress	16. bread
2. aeroplane	7. chair	12. flower	17. pencil
3. lamp	8. horse	13. window	18. curtain
4. cigarette	9. egg	14. perfume	19. vase
5. picture	10. tea cup	15. book	20. hat

Write your score here ___ Score after learning Chapter 6 ___

Test 3

Look at this twenty-digit number for about two and a half minutes, then take a piece of paper and try to write it from memory. Give yourself 5 points for every number that you put down in its correct place or sequence. Understand please that the important thing here is retentiveness, which you cannot test until you have read Chapter 11.

72443278622173987651

Write your score here ___ Score after learning Chapter 11 ___

Test 4

Imagine that someone has taken five cards out of a shuffled pack of playing cards. Now the rest of the cards (47) are called off to you just once. Could you tell, by memory, which five were *not* called, or were missing? Let's try it. Look down this list of forty-seven cards only once. After you've done so, take a pencil and jot down the names of the five cards that you think are missing. You must not look at the book while you are writing. Don't take more than four and a half minutes to look at the list of cards. I will ask you to take this test again, after you have read and studied Chapter 10. Give yourself 20 points for every missing card you list correctly.

Jack Hearts	Three Hearts	Four Spades
Ace Diamonds	Nine Clubs	Queen Spades
King Hearts	Ten Diamonds	Three Clubs
Seven Diamonds	Eight Spades	Jack Clubs
Ten Clubs	Five Spades	Six Hearts
Jack Spades	Ace Spades	Four Hearts
Three Spades	Six Diamonds	Ten Spades
Nine Hearts	Jack Diamonds	King Diamonds
Seven Hearts	Eight Clubs	Ten Hearts
Queen Hearts	Queen Clubs	Queen Diamonds
Three Diamonds	Seven Spades	Eight Diamonds
Two Spades	Seven Clubs	Five Clubs
Ace Clubs	Two Diamonds	Two Clubs
Nine Spades	King Clubs	Five Diamonds
Four Clubs	Eight Hearts	Two Hearts
Five Hearts	Six Spades	

Write your score here ⎯ Score after learning Chapter 10 ⎯⎯

MR GORDON   MR HUNT   MISS SITLER

MR DAEGENSHINE   MR SHAW   MR KORANSKY

MR RUBIN   MR SMALLOWITZ   MISS PALMER

Test 5

Take about six or seven minutes to look at the fifteen faces
and names pictured here. Towards the end of this chapter
you'll find them pictured again in a different order, without
their names. See if you can't give the right name to the right
picture. I'll remind you to take this test again, after you've
read through Chapter 17. Give yourself 5 points for every
name and face that you match up correctly.

Write your score here ⊥⊥ Score after learning Chapter 17 __

MR ENLOVE

MR DONAHUE

MR ZACARIA

MR TALMAN

MISS RALSTONE

MISS CARSON

Test 6

Take seven to nine minutes to look at this list of ten people and their telephone numbers. Then copy all ten people on to a piece of paper, close the book, and see if you can write the telephone number next to each one, from memory. Remember that if you were to dial *one* wrong digit, you would get the wrong party – so, if only one digit in the number is wrong, you get no score on that particular one. I will remind you to take this test again, after you've read through Chapter 19. Give yourself 10 points for each telephone number that you list correctly.

Baker – TA 5-3174	Banker – SU 9-4281
Tailor – RH 3-8295	Mr Karpel – RE 8-9714
Shoemaker – JU 6-0746	Doctor – TA 7-1015
Dentist – WA 4-6904	Mr Goldberg – WA 6-8222
Mr Bookman – CO 5-1127	Mr Corrigan – CA 9-4132

Write your score here __ Score after learning Chapter 19 __

Do not feel discouraged because of the poor marks that you may have received on the foregoing tests. I have given them to you for a definite purpose. First, of course, as I stated

above, that you would be able to see your own progress as you read through this book. Also, to show you how unreliable an untrained memory really is.

It does *not* take a lot of work and study to be able to get 100 per cent on *all* these tests. I like to refer to the system in this book as the 'lazy man's' way of remembering!

4 Interest in memory

The true art of memory is the art of attention. *Samuel Johnson*

Please read the following paragraph very carefully:

You are driving a bus which contains fifty people. The bus makes one stop and ten people get off, while three people get on. At the next stop seven people get off the bus, and two people get on. There are two more stops at which four passengers get off each time, and three fares get on at one stop, and none at the other. At this point, the bus has to stop because of mechanical trouble. Some of the passengers are in a hurry and decide to walk. So eight people get off the bus. When the mechanical trouble is taken care of, the bus goes to the last stop, and the rest of the people get off.

Now, without re-reading the paragraph, see if you can answer two questions about it. I feel pretty sure that if I asked you to tell me how many people were left on the bus, or how many got off the bus at the last stop, you would have the answer immediately. However, one of the questions I want you to answer is: How many stops did the bus make altogether?

I may be wrong, but I don't think that many of you can answer this question. The reason, of course, is that you all felt sure that the question I would ask, after you read the paragraph, would pertain to the number of people. Therefore you gave your attention to the number of people that were getting on and off the bus. You were *interested* in the number of people. In short, you *wanted* to know or remember how many people would be left on the bus. Since you didn't think that the number of stops was important, you didn't pay much attention to that. You weren't interested in the number of stops, therefore they didn't register in your mind at all, and you didn't remember them.

However, if some of you did feel that the number of stops was important or if you felt you *would* be questioned on that particular point, then you surely did know the answer to my first question, or remembered the number of stops that the bus made. Again, simply because you were interested or wanted to know that particular information.

If you feel elated because you did answer my question, don't. Because I doubt if you will answer the second one. A good friend of mine who is employed at Grossingers, a large holiday resort hotel, at which I perform quite often, uses this in his afternoon quizzes. I know that a very small percentage of the guests ever answer this correctly, if at all. Without looking at that first paragraph again, you're to answer this question: What is the bus driver's name?

As I said, I doubt if any of you can answer this correctly, if at all. Actually, this is more of a trick question on observation than it is a memory test. I use it here only to impress upon you the importance of interest in memory. Had I told you before you read that 'bus' story that I would ask for the driver's name – you would have been interested in the name. You'd have *wanted* to notice and remember it.

Even so, it is a tricky sort of question, and you may not have been observant enough to be able to answer it. This, incidentally, is a principle that many professional magicians have been using for years. It is called 'misdirection'. It simply means that the important move in a trick, the move that actually is the *modus operandi*, is kept in the background. Or, it is covered with another move, one that has nothing to do with the trick, but which you are led to believe *is* the important move. This is the move that you will observe and remember. The one that actually worked the trick is not even noticed, and that is why you are completely deceived. Most people, when describing a magician's trick, will make the effect so impossible that if the magician himself were listening, he wouldn't believe it. Only because they leave out the all-important move in their description. Apart from 'box' tricks, or tricks that mechanically work themselves, magicians would have a hard time deceiving their audiences if it weren't for the art of 'misdirection'.

Well, I 'misdirected' you by making you think I was going to ask about one thing, and then I asked about something you didn't even notice. I think I've kept you in suspense long enough. You probably are anxious to know the answer to my second question. Well, actually the *first* word of the paragraph tells you who the driver is. The first word of the paragraph is 'you'. The correct answer to the question, 'What is the bus driver's name?' is *your own name*! *You* were driving the bus. Try this one on your friends and see how few of them can answer it correctly.

As I've said, this is more of an observation test than a memory test. But memory and observation *do* go hand in hand. You cannot possibly remember anything you do not observe; and it is extremely difficult to observe or remember anything that you do not *want* to remember, or that you are not *interested* in remembering.

This, of course, leads to an obvious memory rule. If you want to improve your memory immediately, force yourself to want to remember. Force yourself to be interested enough to observe anything you want to remember or retain. I say 'force yourself', because at first a little effort may be necessary; however, in an amazingly short time you'll find that there is no effort at all required to make yourself want to remember anything. The fact that you are reading this book is your first forward step. You wouldn't be reading it if you didn't want to remember, or if you weren't interested in improving your memory. 'Without motivation there can hardly be remembrance.'

Apart from intending to remember, confidence that you *will* remember is also helpful. If you tackle any memory problem with the thought, 'I will remember', more often than not you will think of your memory as a sieve. Each time that you feel or say, 'I have an awful memory', or, 'I'll never be able to remember this', you put another hole in the sieve. If, on the other hand, you say, 'I have a wonderful memory', or, 'I'll remember this easily', you're plugging up one of those holes.

A lot of people I know invariably ask me why they can't remember a thing, even though they *write* down everything they wish to remember. Well, that's like asking why they can't swim well, even though they tie a twenty-pound stone around their necks. The very fact that they *do* write it is probably why they forget; or rather, why they didn't remember in the first place. As far as I'm concerned, the phrase 'I forgot' should not be in the language. It should be 'I didn't remember in the first place'.

You cannot forget anything you ever really remembered. If you were to write things down with the intent of *aiding* your memory, or with the conscious thought of helping you to be exact with the information, that would be fine. However, using pencil and paper as a substitute for memory (which most people do) is certainly not going to improve it. Your handwriting may improve, or the speed of your writing might improve, but your memory will get worse through neglect and non-use. You see, you usually write things down only because you refuse or are too lazy to take the slight effort or time to remember. Oliver Wendell Holmes put it this way: 'A man must *get* a thing before he can for*get* it.'

Please keep in mind that the memory likes to be trusted. The more you trust it the more reliable and useful it will become. Writing everything down on paper without trying to remember is going against all the basic rules for a stronger and better memory. You're not *trusting* your memory; you haven't the *confidence* in your memory; you're not *exercising* the memory, and your *interest* is not strong enough to retain it, if you must write it down. Remember that you can always lose your paper or notebook, but not your mind. If I may be allowed a small attempt at humour, if you do lose your mind, it doesn't matter much if you remember or not, does it?

Seriously, if you are interested in remembering, if you have confidence that you will remember, you have no need to write everything down. How many parents continually complain that their children have terrible memories, because they can't remember their school work, and consequently get poor marks? Yet, some of these same children can remember the batting averages of every batsman in the county tables. They know all the rules of cricket; or who made what great score in what year for which team, etc. If they can remember these facts and figures so easily and so well, why can't some of them retain their lessons at school? Only because they are more interested in cricket than they are in algebra, history, geography and other school subjects.

The problem is not with their memories, but with their lack of interest. The proof of the pudding is in the fact that most children excel in at least one particular subject, even though they have poor marks in all the others. If a student has a good memory for one subject, he is a good student in that subject. If he can't remember, or has a poor memory in that subject, he will be a poor student in that subject. It's as simple as that. However, this proves that the student *does* have a good memory for things that he likes, or is interested in.

Many of you who went to grammar school had to take a foreign language or two. Do you still remember these languages? I doubt it. If you've travelled in foreign countries, or to places where they speak these particular languages, you've wished many times that you had paid more attention in school. Of course, if you had known that you were going to travel to these places, when you were in school, you would have been interested in learning the language; you would have wanted to do so. You'd have been amazed to find how much better your marks would have been. I know that this is true in my case. If I had known then that I would want to know these languages, I'd have learned and/or remembered much more easily. Unfortunately, I didn't have a trained memory then.

Many women will complain that their memories are atrocious, and that they can't remember a thing. These same women will describe and remember in detail what a lady friend was wearing when they met weeks ago. They can usually spot another woman in a car travelling up to forty miles an hour, and tell you what she's wearing; the colours, her style of hair-do; whether the hair was natural or bleached, and the woman's approximate age!

They'll probably even know how much money this woman had. This, of course, goes out of the realm of memory and starts to touch on psychic powers. The important thing, the thing that I have been trying to stress in this chapter, is that interest is of great importance to memory. If you can remember things that you are interested in to such a tremendous degree, it proves that you do have a good memory. It also proves that if you were as interested in other things, you would be able to remember them just as well.

The thing to do is to make up your mind that you *will* be interested in remembering names, faces, dates, figures, facts – anything; and that you will have confidence in your ability to retain them. This, alone, without the actual systems and methods of associations in this book, will improve your memory to a noticeable degree. *With* the systems of association as an aid to your true memory, you are on your way to an amazingly remarkable and retentive memory. You can start to prove this to yourself in the next chapter.

5 Link method of memory

A man's real possession is his memory. In nothing else is he rich, in nothing else is he poor. *Alexander Smith*

I want to show you now that you can start immediately to remember as you've never remembered before. I don't believe that anyone with an *untrained* memory can possibly remember twenty unassociated items, in sequence, after hearing or seeing them only once. Even though *you* don't believe it either, you will accomplish *just that* if you read and study this chapter.

Before going into the actual memorizing, I must explain that your trained memory will be based almost entirely on *mental pictures* or images. These mental pictures will be easily recalled if they are made as *ridiculous* as you can possibly make them. Here are the twenty items that you will be able to memorize in sequence in a surprisingly short time.

carpet, paper, bottle, bed, fish, chair, window, telephone, cigarette, nail, typewriter, shoe, microphone, pen, television set, plate, doughnut, car, coffee pot, and brick.

A famous man once said that method is the mother of memory. So I'll teach you now what I call the *Link method* of memory. I've told you that your trained memory will consist mostly of ridiculous mental images, so let's make ridiculous mental images of the above twenty items! Don't be alarmed! It is child's play; as a matter of fact it *is* almost like a game.

The first thing you have to do is to get a picture of the first item, 'carpet', in your mind. You all know what a carpet is – so just 'see' it in your mind's eye. Don't just see the word 'carpet', but actually, for a second, see either any carpet, or a carpet that is in your own home and is therefore familiar to you. I have already told you that in order to remember anything, it must be associated in some way to something you already know or remember. You are going to do that right now, and the items themselves will serve as the things you already remember. The thing that you now know or already remember is the item 'carpet'. The new thing, the thing you want to remember will be the second item, 'paper'.

Now then, here is your *first and most important step* towards your trained memory. You must now *associate* or *link* carpet to, or with, paper. The association must be as *ridiculous as possible*. For example, you might picture the carpet in your home made out of paper. See yourself walking on it, and actually hearing the paper crinkle underfoot. You can picture yourself writing something on a carpet *instead* of paper. Either one of these is a ridiculous picture or association. A sheet of paper lying on a carpet would *not* make a good association. It is too logical! Your mental picture *must* be ridiculous or illogical. Take my word for the fact that if your association is a logical one, you will not remember it.

Now, here is the point which I will keep reminding you of throughout this book. You must actually *see* this ridiculous picture in your mind for a fraction of a second. Please do not just try to see the words, but definitely see the *picture* you've decided on. Close your eyes for a second; that might make it easier to see the picture, at first. As soon as you see it, stop thinking about it and go on to your next step. The thing you *now* already know or remember is 'paper', therefore the next step is to associate, or link, paper to the next item on the list, which is 'bottle'. At this point you pay no attention to 'carpet' any longer. Make an entirely new ridiculous mental picture with, or between, bottle and paper. You might see yourself reading a gigantic bottle instead of a paper, or writing on a gigantic bottle instead of on paper. Or you might picture a bottle pouring paper out of its mouth instead of liquid; or a bottle made out of paper instead of glass. Pick the association which *you* think is most ridiculous and *see* it in your mind's eye for a moment.

I cannot stress too much the necessity of actually *seeing* this picture in your mind's eye, and making the mental image as ridiculous as possible. You are not, however, to stop and think for fifteen minutes to find the *most* illogical association; the first ridiculous one that comes to mind is usually the best to use. I'll give you two or more ways in which you might form your pictures with each pair of the twenty items. You are to pick the one that you think is most ridiculous, or one that you've thought of yourself, and use that one association only.

We have already linked carpet to paper, and then paper to bottle. We now come to the next item which is 'bed'. You must make a ridiculous association between bottle and bed. A bottle lying on a bed, or anything like that, would be too logical. So you might picture yourself sleeping in a large bottle instead of a bed, or you might see yourself taking a drink from a bed instead of a bottle. (I can get pretty ridiculous.) See either of these pictures in your mind for a moment, then stop thinking of it.

You realize, of course, that we are always associating the *previous* object to the *present* object. Since we have just used 'bed', this is the previous, or the thing we already know and remember. The present object, or the new thing that we want to remember, is 'fish'. So – make a ridiculous association or link between bed and fish. You could 'see' a giant fish sleeping in your bed; or a bed made out of a gigantic fish. *See* the picture you think is most ridiculous.

Now – 'fish' and 'chair' – see the gigantic fish sitting on a chair, or a large fish being used *as* a chair. Or, you're catching chairs instead of fish while fishing.

Chair and Window – see yourself sitting on a pane of glass (which gives you a pain) instead of a chair. Or you might see yourself violently throwing chairs through a closed window. *See* the picture before going on to the next one.

Window and Telephone – see yourself answering the phone, but when you put it to your ear, it's not a phone you're holding, but a window. Or you might see your window as a large telephone dial, and you have to lift the dial to look out the window. You could see yourself sticking

your hand through a window pane in order to pick up the phone. *See* the picture you think is most ridiculous, for a moment.

Telephone and Cigarette – you're smoking a telephone instead of a cigarette; or you're holding a large cigarette to your ear and talking into it instead of a telephone. Or you might see yourself picking up the phone and a million cigarettes fly out of the mouthpiece and hit you in the face.

Cigarette and Nail – you're smoking a nail; or hammering a lit cigarette into the wall instead of a nail.

Nail and Typewriter – you're hammering a gigantic nail right through a typewriter, or all the keys on your typewriter are nails and they're pricking your fingertips as you type.

Typewriter and Shoe – see yourself wearing typewriters instead of shoes, or you're typing with your shoes. You might want to see a large shoe with keys and you're typing on that.

Shoe and Microphone – you're wearing microphones instead of shoes, or you're broadcasting into a large shoe.

Microphone and Pen – you're writing with a microphone instead of a pen, or you're broadcasting and talking into a giant pen.

Pen and Television Set – you could 'see' a million pens gushing out of the television screen, or pens performing on television, or there is a screen on a gigantic pen and you're (I can't resist this pun) watch-*ink* a television show on it.

Television Set and Plate – picture your television screen as one of your kitchen plates, or see yourself eating out of the television set instead of out of a plate. Or you're eating out of a plate, and seeing a television show in the plate while you eat.

Plate and Doughnut – 'see' yourself biting into a doughnut, but it cracks in your mouth, for it's a plate. Or picture being served dinner in a gigantic doughnut instead of a plate.

Doughnut and Car – you can 'see' a large doughnut driving a car; or see yourself driving a gigantic doughnut instead of a car.

Car and Coffee Pot – a large coffee pot is driving a car, or you're driving a gigantic coffee pot instead of a car. You might picture your car on your stove, with coffee perking in it.

Coffee Pot and Brick – see yourself pouring steaming coffee from a brick instead of a coffee pot, or 'see' bricks pouring from the spout of a coffee pot instead of coffee.

That's it! If you have actually 'seen' these mental pictures in your mind's eye, you will have no trouble remembering the twenty items in sequence, from 'carpet' to 'brick'. Of course, it takes many times the length of time to explain this than to simply do it. Each mental association must be seen for just the smallest fraction of a second, before going on to the next one.

Let's see now if you have remembered all the items. If you were to 'see' a carpet, what would that bring to mind immediate? Why, paper, of course. You saw yourself writing on a carpet, instead of paper. Now, paper brings bottle to mind, because you saw a bottle made of paper. You saw yourself sleeping in a gigantic bottle instead of a *bed*; the bed had a gigantic *fish* sleeping on it; you were fishing, and catching *chairs*, and you were flinging chairs through your closed *window*. Try it! You will see that you will go right through all the items without missing or forgetting any of them.

Fantastic? Unbelievable? Yes! But, as you can see, entirely plausible and possible. Why not try making your own list of objects and memorizing them in the way that you have just learned.

I realize, of course, that we have all been brought up to think logically, and here I am telling you to make illogical or ridiculous pictures. I know that with some of you this may be a bit of a problem at first. You may have a little difficulty in making those ridiculous pictures. However, after doing it for just a little while, the first picture that comes to mind will be a ridiculous or illogical one. Until that happens here are four simple rules to help you.

1. Picture your items *out of proportion*. In other words, too large. In my sample associations for the above items I used the word 'gigantic' quite often. This was to make you get the items *out of proportion*.

2. Picture your items in *action* whenever possible. Unfortunately, it is the violent and embarrassing things that we all remember; much more so than the pleasant things. If you've ever been acutely embarrassed, or been in an accident, no matter how many years ago, you don't need a trained memory to remember it vividly. You still squirm a bit whenever you think of that embarrassing incident that happened years ago, and you probably can still describe in

detail the facts of your accident. So get violent action into your association whenever you can.

3. *Exaggerate* the amount of items. In my sample association between telephone and cigarette, I told you that you might see *millions* of cigarettes flying out of the mouthpiece, and hitting you in the face. If you saw the cigarettes lit and burning your face, you'd have both action and exaggeration in your picture.

4. *Substitute* your items. This is the one that I, personally, use most often. It is simply picturing one item *instead* of another, *i.e.* smoking a nail *instead* of a cigarette.

1. Out of Proportion

2. Action

3. Exaggeration

4. Substitution

Try to get one or more of the above into your pictures, and with a little practice you'll find that a ridiculous association for *any* two items will come to mind instantly. The objects to be remembered are actually linked one to the other, forming a chain, and that is why I call this the *Link* method of remembering. The entire *Link* method boils down to this: associate the first item to the second, the second to the third, third to the fourth, and so on. Make your association as ridiculous and/or illogical as possible, and most important, *See* the pictures in your mind's eye.

In later chapters you will learn some practical applications of the Link system – how it can help you to recall your daily schedule or errands, and how you can use it to help you remember speeches. The Link system is also used to help memorize long digit numbers and many other things. However, don't jump ahead of yourself; don't worry about those things now.

Of course, you can use the Link immediately to help you remember shopping lists, or to show off for your friends. If you want to try this as a memory stunt, have your friend call off a list of objects; have him write them down so that

he can check you. If when you try this you find that you
are having trouble recalling the *first* item, I suggest that you
associate that item to the person that's testing you. For
example, if 'carpet' were the first item, you could 'see' your
friend rolled up in your carpet. Also, if on first trying this
as a stunt, you do forget one of the items, ask what it is and
strengthen that particular association. You either didn't use
a ridiculous enough association, or you didn't *see* it in your
mind, or you would *not* have forgotten it. After you've
strengthened your original association, you'll be able to
rattle off the items from first to last. Try it and see!

The most impressive part of it is that if your friend asks
you to call off the items two or three hours later you will
be able to do it! They will still be brought to mind by your
original associations. If you really want to impress your
listeners, call the items off backwards! In other words, from
the last item called, right up to the first one.

Amazingly enough, this works for you automatically. Just
think of the last item, that will recall the next to last item,
and so on down, or rather, up the line.

By the way, why not try Test 1 in Chapter 3 again.
Compare your score now with the score you had before you
read this chapter on the Link method.

6 Peg system of memory

A certain organization, whose membership consisted of gag-writers only, was having its annual dinner at a swank hotel. One of the membership rules of the organization was that the members would never actually tell a joke or a gag to each other. They had memorized all the standard gags by numbers, and instead of telling the joke, they would save time by simply calling the number of that particular one.

During the dinner, as a situation would present itself, and any of the comedy writers thought of a gag to fit the situation, he would call the number, and shouts of laughter would invariably go up. 'Number 148,' called one – peals of laughter. 'Number 204,' shouted another – more laughter. Towards the end of the dinner one of the new members shouted 'Number 212,' and was greeted by a loud silence. Whereupon his neighbour turned to him and said, 'You'll soon learn, my friend, that it's not the joke that's important, but the *way* you tell it.'

Although the above is pure fiction, most people would say it is impossible to remember so many jokes by number. Let me assure you that it is possible, and I will teach you how, in a later chapter. First, however, you must learn how to remember the numbers. Numbers themselves are about the most difficult things to remember, because they are completely abstract and intangible. It is almost impossible to picture a number. They are geometric designs and they mean nothing in our minds, unless they have been associated to something you know over a period of time. Of course, your own address or your own telephone number does mean something to you. The problem is to be able to associate any and all numbers easily, quickly, and at any time.

If you were to try to hang a painting on your bare living-room wall, what would happen? Why, the painting would fall to the floor, of course. However, if you had a tiny *peg* in that wall, then you would be able to hang the painting on it. What I'm going to do is to give you some 'pegs'; no, not for your wall – but to keep in your mind, always. Anything you wish to remember from now on, having to do with numbers in any way, you will be able to 'hang' on these pegs! That is why I call this the PEG system of memory.

The PEG system will show you how to count with *objects* (which can be pictured) instead of numbers. This is not a particularly new thought. It was first introduced by Stanislaus Mink von Wennsshein along about the year 1648. In the year 1730, the entire system was modified by an Englishman, Dr Richard Grey, who called the idea 'letter' or 'number equivalents'. The idea was sound, but the method just a bit clumsy, because he used vowels as well as consonants in the system. Since 1730, however, many changes have been made, although the idea is basically the same.

In order for you to learn the method, you must first learn a simple *phonetic* alphabet. No need for dismay – it consists of only ten sounds, and with my help it shouldn't take you more than ten minutes to learn them. This will be the most worthwhile ten minutes you've ever spent, since this phonetic alphabet will eventually help you to remember numbers, or numbers in conjunction with anything else, in such a way that you never would have thought possible.

I will give you now a different *consonant sound* for each of the digits 1, 2, 3, 4, 5, 6, 7, 8, 9 and 0. These you must commit to memory. I'll make this simple for you by giving you a 'memory aid' for remembering each one. Read them carefully and with your full attention.

The sound for 1 will always be – T or D. The letter T has *one* downstroke.

The sound for 2 will always be – N. Typewritten n has *two* downstrokes.

The sound for 3 will always be – M. Typewritten m has *three* downstrokes.

The sound for 4 will always be – R. Final sound of the word 'four' is R.

The sound for 5 will always be – L. Roman numeral for 50 is L.

The sound for 6 will always be – J, ch, sh, soft g, etc. The letter J turned around is almost like the number 6. ( ) 6)

The sound for 7 will always be – K, hard c, hard g. The number 7 can be used to form a K. One seven rightside up, and the other upside down. (7K)

The sound for 8 will always be – F or V. Written f and figure 8 both have two loops, one above the other. (ƒ 8)

The sound for 9 will always be – P or B. The number 9 turned around is P.

The sound for 0 (zero) will always be – S or Z. First sound of the word 'zero'.

If you will attempt to picture the little memory aid that I have given with each one, you should remember them easily. Please keep in mind that the letters are not important; we are interested in the sound only. That's why I call this a phonetic alphabet. With some of the digits I've given more than one letter, but the phonetic sounds of these letters are the same, in each case. Your lips, tongue and teeth are used in the same identical way to sound P and B, or F and V, or J, sh, ch, etc. The sound of the letter G in the exclamation 'gee' would, according to the phonetic alphabet, represent 6, whereas the same letter in the word 'go' would represent 7. The letter C in the word 'coat' represents 7, the same letter in the word 'cent' would represent zero, since it is pronounced with the s sound. The letters Kn in the word 'knee' or 'knife' would stand for 2, because the K is silent. Remember then it is the sound that's important, *not* the letter.

Now, look this over once:

1. T, D	6. J, sh, ch, g
2. N	7. K, c, g
3. M	8. F, v
4. R	9. P, b
5. L	0. Z, s

Turn away from this page and see if you remember the sounds from one to zero. Test yourself on remembering them out of order, too. You should know them all by now. I could give you one more aid for memorizing these sounds, by telling you to remember this nonsense phrase: TeN MoRe LoGiC FiBS. This will help you to memorize the sounds in order from one to zero. It is necessary, however, to know them out of sequence – so you shouldn't have to rely on the nonsense phrase too long – the original memory aids that I gave you should suffice.

This simple phonetic alphabet is of utmost importance, and the sounds should be practised until they are second nature to you. Once they are, the rest of the Peg system will be easy for you. Here is a method of practice to help you learn the sounds thoroughly. Any time you see a number, break it down into sounds in your mind. For example, you might see the number 3746 on a car licence plate; you should be able to read it as m, k, r, j. You might see an address 85-29, and be able to read it as fl-np. You can look at any word and practise breaking it down into numbers. The word 'motor' would be 314. The word 'paper' is 994, and 'cigarette' would break down to 0741. (The double tt is the same sound as a single t, therefore it represents 1, not 11.)

None of the vowels a e i o or u have any meaning at all in the phonetic alphabet; neither do the letters w, h or y. (Remember the word, 'why'.)

Before going any further, complete the following exercises. The first column of words should be changed to numbers, and the second column of numbers must be broken into sounds.

climb	7 3 8	6124	TTNR
butler	2 1 5 4	8903	BPSM
chandelier	6 2 1 5 4	2394	NMPR
sounds	0 2 1 0	0567	SLJK
bracelet	8 4 6 5 1	1109	TTSP
hypnotize	8 2 1 0	8374	———

You are ready now to learn some of those 'pegs' I mentioned. I would suggest, however, that you know the sounds thoroughly before you go on to the pegs themselves.

All right, since we now know a certain phonetic sound for all the digits from one to zero, you can see that we can make up a word for any number, no matter how many digits it contains. For example, if we wanted to make up a word for 21, we could use any of the following: net, nut, knot, gnat, nod, neat, note, knit, etc., because they all begin with the n sound (2) and end with the t or d sound (1). For 14 we could use tear, tyre, tore, door, tier, deer, dire, dray, tree, etc., because they all begin with the t or d sound for 1, and end with the r sound for 4. Remember that we are interested in the consonant sounds only.

Do you get the idea of how I formed those words? If you do, then I can go ahead and give you the first few 'pegs'. Each one of the peg words that I will give you has been specially chosen because it is comparatively easy to picture in your mind, and that is important.

Since the number 1 contains only one digit, and that one digit is represented by the t or d sound, we must use a word that contains only that one consonant sound. So we will use the word 'TIE'. From here on in the word 'tie' will always represent the number 1 to you.

As I said, it is important to be able to picture these objects, so I will give explanations of all those where I think an explanation is necessary.

The word 'NOAH' will always represent 2. Picture an old, white-haired man on an ark.

The word 'MA' will always mean 3. Here I suggest that you always picture your own mother.

The word 'RYE' will always represent the number 4. You

can picture either a bottle of Rye whisky *or* a loaf of rye bread. Once you decide on a particular mind picture for this, or for any of the pegs, use that particular picture always. You can see how I arrive at these words. They all have only one consonant sound, and that one sound is the one representing the digit of the number.

The word 'LAW' will always represent 5. The word 'law' itself cannot be pictured; I suggest that you picture any policeman, in uniform, because they represent the law.

Number 6 is the word 'SHOE'. Number 7 is the word 'COW'. Number 8 is the word 'IVY'. For this one you can picture ivy growing all over the sides of a house. Number 9 is the word 'BEE'. Number 10 has *two* digits, the digit 1 and a zero. The peg word for 10 therefore must be made up of a t or d sound and an s or z sound, in that order. We'll use the word 'TOES' – picture your own toes.

Ordinarily it would be a little difficult to remember ten completely unassociated words as I have just given you. Since the peg word for any number *must* contain certain sounds only, you'll find that it is easy. As a matter of fact, if you have read the ten words once, with a little concentration you probably already know them. Try it!

When you say the number to yourself, think of its sound first, then try to remember the peg word. Test yourself in and out of order. You should know that 3 is 'ma', without repeating 'tie', 'Noah', ma!

To show you how fantastic your memory can be with my little memory aids, you can do this until the words become second nature to you. If you come to a number, and you think you can't remember its peg – think of the sound for that number, and say any words that come to your mind, starting with and containing that particular consonant sound only. When you say the right one, it will sort of 'ring a bell' in your mind, and you'll know that that's the right one. For instance, if you couldn't think of the peg word for 1, you might say to yourself 'toy, tow, tea, tie'; as soon as you say 'tie', you'll know that that is the correct word.

You can see, now, what I've done. I have built you up slowly with each item. First I gave you an aid to remember the phonetic sounds, now those sounds are your aid to remember the very important peg words; and the peg words will help you to remember anything where numbers are involved, so make sure you know them well.

1. tie	6. shoe
2. Noah	7. cow
3. ma	8. ivy
4. rye	9. bee
5. law	10. toes

Now, if you feel that you know the first ten peg words thoroughly, I'll show you how to use them for remembering objects in and out of order. I'll give you ten objects, out of sequence, and prove to you that you can remember them after reading them only once!

9 – purse	5 – typewriter
6 – cigarette	2 – television set
4 – ashtray	8 – wrist watch
7 – salt-shaker	1 – fountain pen
3 – lamp	10 – telephone

The first one listed is 9 – purse. All you have to do is to make a ridiculous and/or illogical association of the peg word for 9, which is 'bee', and purse. If you have realized the importance of actually 'seeing' these ridiculous associations in your mind, you'll have no trouble. For this first one, you might see yourself opening a purse and a swarm of bees fly out of it, stinging you. Just 'see' the picture for a moment, then go to the next one.

No. 6 (shoe) – cigarette. You can see yourself smoking a shoe instead of a cigarette, see millions of cigarettes falling out of a shoe, or you can see yourself wearing gigantic cigarettes instead of shoes.

No. 4 (rye) – ashtray. You might see yourself dropping ashes into a scooped-out loaf of rye bread instead of an ashtray, or, you're buttering an ashtray instead of a slice of rye bread.

I am giving you one or more ways that each object can be associated ridiculously with its peg word. You are to use only one of these pictures for each one. Use one that I give, or one that you think of yourself. The first illogical picture that comes to mind is usually the best one to use, because that is the one that will come to mind later on. I'll help you with all ten of them, since it is the first time you are attempting this method; but after this you should be able to do it without my help.

No. 7 (cow) – salt-shaker. Picture yourself milking a cow, but the cow has salt-shakers instead of udders. Or see salt-shakers coming out instead of milk.

No. 3 (ma) – lamp. You can picture your mother wearing a gigantic lamp for a hat. See the lamp going on and off. (Action – Rule 2.)

No. 5 (law) – typewriter. You might 'see' a policeman putting handcuffs on a typewriter, or you can see a typewriter walking the beat, swinging a truncheon, like a policeman.

No. 2 (Noah) – television set. You might picture Noah sailing on a television set instead of an ark.

No. 8 (ivy) – wrist watch. You can see millions of wrist watches growing all over the side of your house, instead of ivy; or, you can see yourself wearing ivy on your wrist instead of a watch.

No. 1 (tie) – fountain pen. Picture yourself wearing a gigantic fountain pen instead of a tie, or you might see yourself writing with your tie, instead of a fountain pen.

No. 10 (toes) – telephone. See yourself dialling with your toes, or, you pick up the telephone, but it turns out that you're holding your toes. (Probably talking to a heel.)

Now – take a piece of paper, number it from one to ten, and try to fill in the objects in order, without looking at the book. When you come to 1, just picture your peg word, tie, and the ridiculous picture of you wearing a fountain pen instead of a tie will come back to you immediately. So you know that 1 is fountain pen. When you picture Noah, you will see him on a television set instead of an ark; so you know that 2 is a television set.

You will remember them all quite easily. The wonderful part about it is that you also know them out of sequence. You can see, of course, that it makes no difference. You can also call them off backwards – just think of the peg word for 10 (toes) and work up to 'tie'.

You should now be thoroughly amazed at your own ability. But wait! Why not memorize twenty-five objects instead of only ten? Well, at the end of this chapter you will find the peg words for numbers 11 through to 25. Please learn those just as you learned the first ten. When you know them perfectly, try this on your friend. Have him number a sheet of paper from one to twenty or twenty-five, or as many as you wish to show off with. Then have him call out any of those numbers, haphazardly, and then name any tangible object. Ask him to write that object alongside the number called. Have him do that until every number has an object next to it. Now call them right back to him from 1 right down to the last one. Then have him call any number, and you immediately give him the object, or have him call any object and you tell him what number it is!

Don't let that last part bother you, there is nothing to it. If I were to ask you now what number salt-shaker was, you would 'see' the ridiculous picture of a *cow* with salt-shakers instead of udders. Since 'cow' is the peg for 7, then you know that salt-shaker was 7.

Watch the look of astonishment on your pal's face when you finish!

Please do not go on to the next chapter until you are sure that you know all the peg words from 1 to 25.

11. tot	15. towel	19. tub	23. name
12. tin	16. dish	20. nose	24. Nero
13. tomb	17. tack	21. net	25. nail
14. tyre	18. dove	22. nun	

For 'tot', it is best to picture a child that you know. For 12, you can see the object called, made out of 'tin'. For 'tomb', picture a gravestone. For 20, you can see the object called, on your face in place of your 'nose'. For 'net', you can use either a fishing net, a hair net, or a tennis net.

For 23, you can see the object you wish to remember forming your 'name'. For instance, if the object were cigarette, you would picture your own name printed out very large with cigarettes. If you don't care for that idea, you might picture one of your business cards for 'name', or any other possession that has your name on it. Whatever you decide on, you must use it all the time. For 'Nero', I always picture a man playing a fiddle.

Remember, please, that once you decide on a particular picture for any of the peg words, you are to use that picture all the time.

If you know the pegs from 1 to 25 thoroughly (and I suggest that you go no further until you do), and if you feel confident (or even if you don't), why not take Test 2 in Chapter 3 once again. Try it, and then compare your present score with the original one!

7 Uses of the peg and link systems

NEW PATIENT: 'Doctor, I don't know what to do. You've got to help me; I just can't remember a thing. I've no memory at all. I hear something one minute, and the next minute, I forget it! Tell me, what should I do?'
DOCTOR: 'Pay in advance!'

I can't blame the doctor for wanting his fee in advance in the above anecdote; but I guess that most of us who forget to pay bills do so because we don't *want* to remember them. According to Austin O'Malley, 'A habit of debt is very injurious to the memory.' Unfortunately, we are usually soon reminded of debts.

If you've grasped the idea behind the Link and the Peg systems of memory, you have learned two of the three things that your trained memory will be based upon. The third is the system of substitute words or substitute thoughts, which I will discuss in later chapters.

You can start applying what you've learned immediately, if you want to. Not particularly for remembering debts, which I'm sure you'd rather forget, but perhaps for memorizing the errands that you have to do for each day. If you usually write out your shopping list, why not try to memorize it with the help of the Link system. Simply link the first item to the second item, the second to the third, and so on, down the list. You can memorize an entirely different list the next time you go shopping without fear of confusion. The beautiful thing about the Link method is that you can forget a list whenever you wish. Actually, when you memorize the second shopping list, the first one fades away. You can, of course, retain as many lists or links as you desire.

The mind is a most fantastic machine; it can be compared

to a filing cabinet. If you have memorized a list of items with the Link system, which you want to retain – you can. If you want to forget the list – you can. It is merely a question of desire. The list that you want to remember is one which you probably intend to use, or you would have no reason to retain it. The use of the list itself will tend to etch it into your memory. If it happens to be a list that you do not intend to utilize right away, but which you feel you want to retain for future use – you can do that, too. You would have to go over the list in your mind the day after you memorized it. Then go over it again a few days later. After doing this a few times, you have filed the list away, and it will be ready when you need it.

We all realize, of course, that it is sometimes necessary to forget! Benjamin Disraeli, when asked about the favour shown him by royalty, said, '—I observe a simple rule of conduct; I never deny; I never contradict; I sometimes forget.' This, however, is a question of diplomacy, not memory; and I know that you're reading this book not to be taught how to forget, but how to remember. I will show you soon how to use the Link system to remember speeches, articles, anecdotes, etc.

The main difference between the Link and the Peg methods is that the Link is used to remember anything in sequence, while the Peg is for memorizing things in and out of order. You may feel that you have no need for the Peg system since you don't have to remember anything out of order. Believe me when I tell you that you definitely should learn the Peg system thoroughly. It will be extremely useful for remembering telephone numbers, pattern numbers, long digit numbers, addresses – as a matter of fact, the Peg system will aid you in remembering *anything* that has to do with numbers in any way. Besides, it will enable you to do some fantastic memory stunts for your friends.

Although I intend to go deeper into memorizing schedules or appointments for the week, day or month, in later chapters – I can show you how to apply what you have already learned to this problem, right now. You can use either the Peg or Link methods, or one in conjunction with the other.

Let's assume that you have the following errands to do on one particular day: you have to have your car washed (now we know that it must rain today); make a deposit at the bank; post a letter; see your dentist; pick up the umbrella that you forgot at a friend's house (you hadn't read the chapter on absent-mindedness, as yet); buy some perfume for your wife; call or see the television repair man; stop at the hardware shop for bulbs, a hammer, a picture frame, an extension cord and an ironing board cover; go to the bookseller to buy a copy of this book for a forgetful friend; have your watch repaired; and finally, bring home one dozen eggs. (My, but you've got a busy day!)

Now, as I've said, you can use the Link or Peg systems to enable you to remember to do each of the above errands. Using the Link method: simply make a ridiculous picture between car and bank – you might see yourself driving into the bank in your recently washed car; you're depositing *letters* instead of money; now picture your *dentist* pulling letters out of your mouth instead of teeth – or he's using a letter instead of a drill. To remember the errand concerning the umbrella – picture your dentist working over you while he's holding an umbrella over his head; make a ridiculous picture between umbrella and perfume, now, perfume to television; television to hardware; hardware to book; book to watch; and finally, watch to eggs.

I've given you examples with the first few errands only, because I want you to use your own imagination for forming ridiculous mental links. You simply do the same as if you were linking a list of objects. Actually it is the same thing – when you come to the watch repairing and the purchase of the dozen eggs, it isn't necessary to get the *repairing* or *amount* of eggs into the picture. Just use watch and egg for your ridiculous picture: i.e. you're breaking an egg, and a wrist watch falls out; or you're wearing an egg instead of a wrist watch. The one item will bring the entire errand to mind, of course. These are just memory aids or reminders;

you already have remembered that you must repair the watch or that it is a dozen eggs that you need. Thinking of, or being reminded of watch and egg is all that is necessary to start you off on your errand.

When you get to the hardware shop, you have to buy five items. Make a *separate* link of these five: you can start by 'seeing' a large *bulb* as the proprietor of the shop; you break him with a *hammer*; you *frame* a hammer and hang it on your wall, and so on, to ironing board cover.

After you have linked all your errands for the day, all you have to do is complete one, and that will remind you of the next, and so on. However, you needn't do all these errands in sequence just because you used the Link method to remember them. That might make it a little inconvenient, unless you've arranged your errands accordingly. No, you can do them in any order you like. Each time you complete an errand, go over the link in your mind, in order to remind yourself if there is one that is convenient to take care of at that moment, considering the time and place. When you think you have attended to all your duties for the day, go over the Link, and if there is one you've missed, you'll know it immediately.

You can utilize the Peg system, of course, for the same thing. Just associate washing the car with your peg word for 1 (tie). You might picture yourself wearing a car instead of a tie. Now, associate

bank to Noah (2)
letter to ma (3)
dentist to rye (4)
umbrella to law (5)
perfume to shoe (6)
television to cow (7)
hardware to ivy (8)
book to bee (9)
watch to toes (10)
eggs to tot (11)

Use the Link to remember the different items you want at the hardware shop. You could even use the Peg for this by making another set of associations, i.e. bulb to tie; hammer to Noah, etc. They wouldn't conflict at all, but it is easier to use the Link.

Now, again, when you're ready to start the day, think of your peg for 1 (tie). This will remind you that you have to get the car washed. When that's done, think of your peg for 2 (Noah) and that will remind you to go to the bank, etc. You don't have to do these in order, either; simply keep going over the pegs, and if you've forgotten something, it'll stand out like an eagle in a canary cage.

There you have it! No more excuses to the wife that you forgot to wash the car, or that you forgot to buy the eggs. As I mentioned before, we'll go further into methods for remembering schedules and appointments in another chapter; wherein you will learn to remember appointments for definite times and days. For the time being what you've learned in this chapter will suffice for simple errands. Before going to bed each night, list your errands and appointments for the following day. Memorize them as explained, then go over them in the morning just to make sure. That's all there is to it.

Before completing this chapter, please learn the pegs for 26 to 50. These, of course, follow the rules of the phonetic alphabet, as do all the pegs.

26. notch	35. mule	43. ram
27. neck	36. match	44. rower
28. knife	37. mug	45. roll
29. knob	38. movie	46. roach
30. mice	39. mop	47. rock
31. mat	40. rose	48. roof
32. moon	41. rod	49. rope
33. mummy	42. rain	50. lace
34. mower		

If the item to be associated with 26 were cigarette, you could see a gigantic cigarette with a 'notch' in it. For 'mower', picture a lawn-mower. For 'mug', picture a beer mug. You can use either a fishing rod or a curtain rod for 41. In associating the word for 42, 'rain', I usually picture it raining the particular item that I want to recall. For 'roll', you might use a breakfast roll.

Be sure that you know all the words from one to fifty, thoroughly, before reading any further. You should know the higher numbered words as well as the lower ones. A good way to practise this would be to remember a list of twenty-five objects, in and out of sequence, using the peg words from *26 to 50* to do it. Just number the paper from 26 to 50 instead of 1 to 25. After a day or so, if you feel ambitious, you can try a list of fifty items. If you make sure that you use strong, ridiculous associations, you shouldn't have any trouble remembering all of them.

8 How to train your observation

```
┌─────────────────────────────┐
│                             │
│        PARIS                │
│                             │
│         IN                  │
│                             │
│     THE    THE              │
│                             │
│        SPRING               │
│                             │
│          x                  │
│                             │
└─────────────────────────────┘
```

Have you looked at the phrase in the box on top of this page? If you have, read it again to make sure that you know what it says. Now turn your head away from the book and repeat the phrase. Check it again to see if you have it right! Some of you will probably think it's a bit silly for me to ask you to keep making sure of a simple phrase like that, but it's important for you to be absolutely aware of what it says.

Now – if you've looked at it closely at least three times; what *does* it say? Does it say, 'Paris in the spring'? I guess that most of you are nodding, 'Yes, of course, that's what it says.' Well, at the risk of being repetitious, check it again will you?

Have you looked at it again? If you *still* think it reads 'Paris in the spring' your observation is not as keen as it should be. If you will check it once more, and this time point to each word as you read the phrase, you will be amazed to discover that it reads, 'Paris in *the the* spring'! There is one 'the' too many in the phrase!

Now you see why I asked you to look at it repeatedly. I wanted to prove that you could look at it any number of times and still not notice the extra 'the'. If you did notice it right away, don't feel too elated. I honestly didn't know whether this little stunt would be as effective when it appeared on top of a page of print, as when used by itself. You see, I've tested hundreds of people with this, and only one or two spotted it quickly. Prove it to yourself by printing it just exactly as I have it, on a 3 × 5 index card, or on a piece of paper of similar size. The little x under the word 'spring' is just misdirection. It tends to draw the readers' eyes down to it, and their minds jump ahead on the phrase itself, because it is such a familiar one. Make one and try it with your friends. I've had people look at it as many as ten or fifteen times, and they were willing to bet anything that they knew just what it said. You can ask them to read aloud directly from the card, and they still say, 'Paris in the spring'!

I am discussing this only to show that the sense of observation could stand a little sharpening, for most of us. As I said earlier in the book, although my systems actually *force* you to observe *if* you apply them – your sense of observation can be strengthened with a little practice. If you're interested in helping your memory, don't sell observation short. You just can't remember anything that you do not observe to begin with. Educationalist Eustace H. Miles said about the same thing, 'What one has never properly realized, one cannot properly be said to remember either.' If you haven't observed, then you haven't realized, and what you haven't realized you *can't* forget, since you never really remembered it in the first place.

If you want to take the time, it is a simple matter to strengthen your sense of observation. You can start right now! You're probably reading this at home, sitting in a room that should be thoroughly familiar to you. Take a piece of paper, and without looking around you, list *everything* in the room. Don't leave out anything you can think of, and try to describe the entire room in detail. List every ashtray, every piece of furniture, pictures, ornaments, etc. Now, look around the room and check your list. Notice all the things you did not put down on your list, or never really observed, although you have seen them countless times. Observe them now! Step out of the room and test yourself once more. Your list should be longer this time. You might try the same thing with other rooms in your home. If you keep at this, your observation will be keener no matter where you happen to be.

You've all heard, I'm sure, of the little experiment that a college professor tried with his students. He had a violent murder scene enacted in front of them, without letting them know that it was just an act. All of the students were told that they must act as witnesses, and were told to describe, in detail, what they saw. Of course, all descriptions varied, even down to what the murderer looked like. All the students in the class had *seen* the same thing, but their observation and their memories were faulty.

This was proven again quite recently in the U.S.A. by popular entertainer, Steve Allen, on his TV show, 'Tonight'. Some members of his cast suddenly burst in, in front of the cameras, enacting a wild, violent scene. Some shots were fired (blanks, of course), clothes were torn, and so on. The whole thing lasted perhaps a minute. Then Mr Allen had three members of the audience come up to attempt to answer some pertinent questions about the scene. He asked how many shots were fired, who was shooting at whom, colour of clothing, etc. All the answers varied and nobody seemed quite sure of anything. As a matter of fact, when Steve asked Skitch Henderson (who had fired the shots) how many shots he had fired – Skitch wasn't too sure himself.

Of course, you can't go around looking for violent scenes to observe – but you can practise in this way. Think of someone whom you know very well. Try to picture his or her face; now see if you can describe the face on paper. List everything you can possibly remember. Go into detail – list colour of hair and eyes, complexion, any or all outstanding features, whether or not they wear glasses, what type of glasses, type of nose, ears, eyes, mouth, forehead, approximate height and weight, hairline, on which side is the hair parted, is it parted at all, etc., etc. The next time you see this person, check yourself. Note the things you didn't observe and those you observed incorrectly. Then try it again! You will improve rapidly.

A good way to practise this is in the underground or bus, or any public conveyance. Look at one person for a moment, close your eyes and try to mentally describe every detail of this person's face. Pretend that you are a witness at a criminal investigation, and your description is of utmost importance. Then look at the person again (don't stare, or you *will* be in a criminal investigation) and check yourself. You'll find your observation becoming more detailed each time you try it.

One last suggestion as to a form of practice. Look at any shop window display. Try to observe everything in it (without using the Peg or Link systems). Then list all the items without looking at the display. You can wait until you're home to do this; then go back to check, when you can. Note the items you left out and try it again. When you think you've become proficient at it, try remembering the prices of the items also.

Each time you do any of these exercises, your sense of observation will become noticeably sharper. Although all this is not absolutely necessary for the acquiring of a trained memory, it is a simple matter to strengthen your observation. If you take the little time to practise, you will soon begin to observe better, *automatically*.

Before reading any further, I would suggest that you memorize the Peg Words from 51 to 75. I might also suggest that for the time being, you use the words that I give you. You could, of course, make up your own words, as long as they stay in the phonetic alphabet system. These would probably serve you just as well, but you might pick some words that would conflict with some of the words that you will eventually learn for other purposes. So, wait until you've finished the book, and then change words to your heart's content.

51. lot	60. cheese	68. chef
52. lion	61. sheet	69. ship
53 loom	62. chain	70. case
54. lure	63. chum	71. cot
55. lily	64. cherry	72. coin
56. leech	65. jail	73. comb
57. log	66. choo choo	74. car
58. lava	67. chalk	75. coal
59. lip		

For 'lot', picture an auction sale. For 'loom', you might find it easier to picture a spinning wheel. 'Lure' is bait for fishing; you might picture a worm. For 'chum', you can picture a particularly close friend; if you do, use the same friend each time. 'Choo choo' is a train, of course. For 'chef', picture a chef's hat. For 'case', see a large wooden packing crate, or a suitcase.

9 It pays to remember speeches, articles, scripts and anecdotes

The confused and nervous speaker was introduced after dinner. He approached the microphone and murmured haltingly:
'My f-f-friends, wh-when I arrived here this evening only God and I knew what I was going to say to you. And now, only God knows!'

I guess that one of the most embarrassing things that can happen to a person is to forget a speech while in front of his audience. Next to forgetting the speech is the embarrassment of faltering along as if you're not sure of what you have to say. Actually, it seems to me that anyone who is asked to give a talk on any particular subject must know that subject pretty well; otherwise why would he be asked to talk about it? No; speakers who falter or hesitate during their speeches, do so, I think, because they have forgotten the next word – or because they are fearful that they *will* forget the next word.

There, in my opinion, lies the problem. If a speech is memorized word for word, and then a word, here and there, is forgotten, it surely will not be delivered as it should be. Why should you have to grope for one particular word? If you can't think of it; why, use any other word that serves the same purpose. Isn't that much better than humming and hawing until you remember the exact phrasing just the way you memorized it?

The people who realized this felt that the next best thing would be to simply read the speech. This solves the problem of forgetting words, until you lose your place on the paper, and forget what you're talking about altogether. Besides, it seems to me that there is a subtle annoyance evident in an audience that is listening to someone reading a speech word for word. I know I feel that way; he might just as well have given me a printed copy of the speech to read at my own leisure.

So, the next step seems to be not to prepare at all. Well, not quite. Even if you are well versed in your subject, you may forget some of the facts you want to speak about. As in the case of the itinerant preacher who always complained that he made his best speeches on the way home. All that he had forgotten to tell his listeners came to mind then, and his horse usually got the best part of the speech.

I believe that the best way to prepare a speech is to lay it out thought for thought. Many of our better speakers do just that. They simply make a list of each idea or thought that they want to talk about, and use this list in lieu of notes. In this way, you can't forget words, since you haven't memorized any. You can hardly lose your place; one glance at your list will show you the next thought to put into words.

But, for those of you who would rather not rely on pieces of paper – the Link method can help you easily. If you wish to memorize your speech thought for thought, from the beginning to the end, you would be forming a *sequence*. That's why you would use the Link method to memorize it.

I would suggest that you go about it something like this: First, write out or read the entire speech. When you're satisfied with it, read it over once or twice more to get the gist of it. Now, get a piece of paper and start to list your KEY WORDS

Read the first thought of the speech. This might be contained in one, two or more sentences; it doesn't matter. Now select *one* word or phrase from these sentences which you think will bring the entire thought to mind! That is not at all difficult. In every sentence or paragraph there *must* be one word or phrase which will remind you of the entire thought. That one word or phrase is your Key Word.

After you have found the Key Word for the first thought, find one for the next thought, and so on. When you're through with the whole speech, you'll have a list of Keys to remind you of each thing you want to say. Actually, if you were to keep this list in front of you as you made the speech, it would serve the purpose. But, if you've mastered the Link system, you know that it is just as easy to make a link of these Key Words, and then throw away the paper.

You might, for example, be giving a talk on your local school problems at a Parent–Teacher Association meeting. Your list of Key Words might look something like this: crowds, teachers, fire, furniture, subjects, playground, etc. In other words, you wish to start your speech with a reference to the *crowded* conditions in the classrooms. Then you want to talk about the *teachers*; perhaps about methods and salaries, etc. Now, you express your thoughts on *fire* drills and fire precautions, which leads you into your discussion on the state of the school's *furniture*; the desks, chairs, blackboards, equipment, and so on. Now, you would talk about your ideas on the *subjects* taught, and finally, the recreation (*playground*) facilities of the school.

You can see that if you make a link: crowd associated to teacher; teacher to fire; fire to furniture, etc., each thought would lead you to the next one, right through to the end of your speech!

At first, you may have to list, perhaps, two or three Key Words for some thoughts. List as many of them as you need, to remember the entire speech. As you use this idea, the amount of Keys necessary will be less and less. And, most important, the confidence you gain by *knowing* that you remember your talk will show when you deliver it. Just keep in mind that you must take care of the thoughts; the words will take care of themselves!

If, for some reason or other, you wish to memorize a speech word for word, use the same method. You'll just have to go over it more often. Remember that all these systems are aids to your true memory. 'If you remember the main, the incidentals will fall into place.' You actually never forget anything you've remembered, you just have to be reminded of it; the system in this book will do that for you. So, if you remember the *main* thoughts of your speech, the incidentals, the ifs, ands and buts, will fall into place.

The same ideas are used to memorize any article you read,

if you desire. First read the article, of course, to get the gist of it. Then pick out the Key Words for each thought; then make a link to remember them, and you've got it. With a bit of practice, you'll actually be able to do this *as* you read.

Many times while reading for enjoyment, I'll come across some piece of information that I'd like to remember. I simply make a conscious association of it, while I'm reading. This idea can, if used enough, speed up your reading considerably. I think that most people are slow readers because by the time they've reached the third paragraph, they've forgotten what was in the first; so they have to jump back.

There is no need to associate everything; just the points that you feel are necessary to remember. Perhaps, if you use my systems, you will fall into the first class of readers in American educationalist William Lyon Phelps's two classes. He once said, 'I divide all readers into two classes; those who read to remember and those who read to forget.'

The same system of linking Key Words can be used for remembering lyrics and scripts. Of course, in this case it is usually necessary to memorize them word for word. You will have to go over them more often, but the Key Word idea will make the job so much easier for you. If you have trouble memorizing your cues in a play, why not associate the last word of the other actor's line to the first word of your line. Even if your cue tells you that you must perform an action, instead of speaking a line, you can still associate it. If the last word of the line prior to your action happens to be, say, 'walk'; and the script calls for you to stoop down to pick up a cigarette end – make a picture in your mind of yourself *walking* along and continually stooping to pick up cigarette ends. (In this way you will never walk on another actor's lines.)

I'll mention one other use of the Key Word idea, before leaving it entirely. How many times have you wanted to tell your friends some jokes or anecdotes that you recently heard, only to find that you've forgotten them completely? You can hear a whole batch of really funny stories one day, and have them all, or most of them, slip your mind the next. Well, according to Irvin S. Cobb, 'A good storyteller is a person who has a good memory and hopes other people haven't.'

Your memory for stories and anecdotes will improve immediately if you use the Key Word system. Just take one word from the story, a word from the punch line is usually best, that will bring the entire joke to mind. When you get your Key Words, you can either link them to each other to remember all the stories in sequence, or use the Peg system to remember them by number.

Perhaps you've heard the gag that has been making the rounds recently about the Flying Saucer that landed in America. Out stepped a creature from outer space – brushed himself off with one of his six arms, looked around with the one large eye in the centre of his forehead, and kept his antennae alert for any sounds.

After exploring a bit, he finally approached a garage, walked over to the petrol pump, saluted, and demanded, 'Take me to your President!'

Well, if you hadn't heard this before, and wanted to remember it with perhaps ten or twelve other stories – you could use either flying saucer, creature from outer space or

petrol pump as your Key Word for this story. Any one of these would surely bring the entire story to mind, *if* you liked it in the first place.

Although I'm sure that many of you will find some practical use for it, one of the memory stunts I sometimes use in my shows is the 'magazine test'. This usually causes a bit of comment because it seems to be the most amazing of memory feats. Actually it is basic and simple.

What happens is this: the audience is given some copies of a current magazine. They are then asked to call any page number, and I immediately tell them the highlights of that particular page.

This is merely another use of the Peg system of memory. In some instances the Link method is used in conjunction with the Peg, as will be explained directly. To memorize the pages of any picture magazine, all you have to do is to associate the peg word that represents the page number to the highlight of that page.

For example: if Page 1 has a picture of an aeroplane on it, you would make a ridiculous association between 'tie' (1) and aeroplane.

Page 2 might be an advertisement for shoe polish. Associate 'Noah' to shoe polish.

Page 3 has a picture of a horse on it. Associate 'ma' to horse.

Page 4 might have a picture of a circus scene; just associate 'rye' to circus.

Page 5 is an advertisement for a television set. Associate 'law' to television set.

Page 6 is a book review. Associate 'shoe' to book.

That's all there is to it. If you go over the magazine and your associations two or three times, you will know the highlights of every page. If a page has more than one picture on it, use the Link method to remember them. Assume that Page 14 is a fashion page, and it has a picture of a hat, one of gloves and a third of a dress.

First associate 'tyre' (14) to the first picture, which is of a hat. Now, link hat to gloves, and then gloves to dress. When

Page 14 is called, the peg word will remind you of hat; hat will tell you that the next picture is of gloves, and gloves will remind you of dress.

If you have seen my performance, you know that I also tell the audience on what part of the page the picture is located; whether it is on the lower or upper left part of the page, upper or lower right, or centre, etc. Well, you can do this too, and without any extra effort.

As I've already mentioned, your normal or true memory does most of the work for you; these systems are just aids that make it easier. As you use my systems you'll find your true memory getting stronger. The best example of this is in memorizing a magazine. In order to make the associations in the first place, you must really see and observe the picture on the page. Because of this, when any page number is called, the peg word for that number acts as an aid to enable you to almost reproduce the entire page in your mind's eye. You will *know* on what part of the page the picture is located. You can only prove this to yourself by trying it.

The only thing you will not be able to do as yet is to remember the names of any people pictured on the pages. This problem will be solved for you after you've read the chapters on remembering names and faces, and how to utilize *substitute words or thoughts*.

Before reading any further, learn the last of the one hundred peg words.

76. cage	85. file	93. bump
77. coke	86. fish	94. bear
78. cave	87. fog	95. bell
79. cob	88. fife	96. beach
80. fez	89. fob	97. book
81. fit	90. bus	98. puff
82. phone	91. bat	99. pipe
83. foam	92. bone	100. thesis *or* disease
84. fur		

For 'cob', picture corn on the cob. For 'fit', you can picture an epileptic fit, or a girdle (tight fit). For 'file', you can use either a filing cabinet or a nail file. 'Fob' is a watch fob. For 'bat', picture a cricket bat. For 'puff', picture a lady's powder puff, and for 'pipe' see a man's smoking pipe.

After learning these, you should be able to count from one to one hundred quickly, with your peg words only. The beauty of it is that you don't have to take time out to practise them. If you're travelling to work, or doing anything that doesn't require thought – you can go over all the pegs in your mind. If you go over them just every once in a while, they'll soon be as familiar to you as the numbers from one to one hundred.

10 It pays to remember playing cards

'Yes, my grandfather was a gambler,
and he died at a very early age.'
'That's too bad. How did it happen?'
'He died of five Aces!'

Since I want you all to stay healthy, the memory feats in this
lesson utilize an ordinary pack of cards; not with five, but
with the usual four Aces. Truthfully, although this chapter
is devoted entirely to remembering playing cards, I am
stressing the *demonstrations* you can do with a pack of cards
and your trained memory. The systems, however, can be
applied to many card games. Please don't think that after
you've mastered these you can always win at cards. Keep in
mind that you can't beat a man at his own game. I will
leave the applications of the systems up to you; I use them
for demonstration purposes only.

The late Damon Runyon used the following in one of his
stories: ' "Son," the old guy says, "no matter how far you
travel, or how smart you get, always remember this: Some
day, somewhere, a guy is going to come to you and show you
a nice brand new pack of cards on which the seal is never
broken, and this guy is going to offer to bet you that the
Jack of Spades will jump out of this pack and squirt cider in
your ear."

' "But, son," the old guy says, "do not bet him, for as sure
as you do you are going to get an ear full of cider." ' '

The memory stunts you will do with cards after studying
these methods will seem almost as amazing to your friends.
Apart from that, they are also wonderful memory exercises.
I suggest that you read and learn the contents of this chapter
whether or not you indulge in card playing.

Cards, of course, are difficult to picture, just as numbers were before you started reading this book. In order for you to be able to remember them, I'll show you how to *make* them mean something; something that you *can* picture in your mind. Some years ago I read an article in a popular magazine about a professor who was trying some sort of experiment. He was attempting to teach people how to memorize the order of a shuffled pack of cards. The article mentioned the fact that he had accomplished his goal. After *six months* of training, his students were able to look at a mixed pack for *twenty minutes or more*, and then call off the cards. I don't know the exact system that was used, but I do know that it had something to do with seeing the cards actually laid out in order, in the mind. I have nothing against this; it's just that it shouldn't take you more than a day or two at the most to learn my system. When you have mastered it, it won't take twenty minutes to memorize a shuffled pack of cards. It might take about ten minutes at first, and with time and practice, you'll cut it down to five minutes!

There are actually two things that you must know in order to remember cards. First is a list of at least fifty-two peg words for the numbers 1 to 52; these you already know. You also have to know a peg word for every card in a pack of cards. These card peg words are not chosen at random. As with the number pegs, they are selected because they are easy to picture, and because they follow a definite system. Here it is, in a nutshell:

Barring a few exceptions which will be discussed later, every card peg word will begin with the initial letter of the card *suit*, i.e. all the words for the Spade suit will begin with the letter 'S'; all the words for the Diamond suit will begin with the letter 'D'; the Club suit – with 'C', and the Heart suit with 'H'. Each word will end with a consonant sound; this sound will represent the numerical value of the card, according to our phonetic alphabet.

You can see then that the word you use *must* represent only one particular card. The first letter will give you the suit, the last sound will give you the value. Let me give you some examples: the peg word for the Two of Clubs must begin with the letter 'C', and must end with the N sound, which represents 2. Of course, there are many words that would fall into this category; cone, coin, can, cane, etc. I've selected the word 'can'. 'Can' will always represent the Two of Clubs! Which card would the word 'hog' stand for? Well, it could represent only one card. It begins with 'H', therefore it's a Heart; it ends with the hard 'g' sound, which represents 7 – 'hog' is the peg word for the Seven of Hearts. Can you think of a word for the Six of Diamonds? Well, it has to begin with a 'D' and end with the J or sh sound – we'll use the word 'dash' to represent the Six of Diamonds.

Here are all fifty-two card peg words. Look them over carefully, and I assure you that you can know and retain them with no more than perhaps twenty minutes to a half-hour of study. Look them over once, then read on for the explanation of the exceptions, and how to picture some of the words. Towards the end of this chapter I'll give you a method to enable you to learn these words thoroughly.

Clubs	Hearts	Spades	Diamonds
AC – cat	AH – hat	AS – suit	AD – date
2C – can	2H – hone	2S – sun	2D – dune
3C – comb	3H – hem	3S – sum	3D – dam
4C – core	4H – hare	4S – sore	4D – door
5C – coal	5H – hail	5S – sail	5D – doll
6C – cash	6H – hash	6S – sash	6D – dash
7C – cock	7H – hog	7S – sock	7D – dock
8C – cuff	8H – hoof	8S – safe	8D – dive
9C – cap	9H – hub	9S – soap	9D – deb
10C – case	10H – hose	10S – suds	10D – dose
JC – club	JH – heart	JS – spade	JD – diamond
QC – cream	QH – queen	QS – steam	QD – dream
KC – king	KH – hinge	KS – sing	KD – drink

The exact system for forming the card pegs has been used for the Aces to Tens only. The reason for this should be obvious to you. If we were to follow the same system for the court, or picture cards, each court card peg word would have to contain two consonant sounds apart from the first letter. This is so because the Jack represents 11, the Queen 12, and the King 13. It would be a bit difficult to find words that are easy to picture, and which would still fit into the system. So, for the four Jacks I simply use the name of the suit itself for the peg word; each of which is a word that is easily pictured. The King of Clubs and Queen of Hearts will always be represented by the words 'king' and 'queen' respectively. For the remaining court cards I have chosen words that begin with the initial suit letter, and that *rhyme* as closely as possible to the sound of the card itself, i.e. King (Spades) – sing: Queen (Diamonds) – dream.

Don't let these exceptions confuse you, they'll stay in your mind because of the fact that they *are* exceptions.

If you have looked at the list of card pegs, you have undoubtedly recognized some of them as being the same as your number words. This will not create any confusion since the duplications only occur with words *over* 52 in your pegs. Being that there are only fifty-two cards in a pack, the words will never conflict.

You are to do the same with the card words as you did with the number pegs. Select a certain mind picture for each word, and use that picture all the time. For the word 'core', you might picture the core of an apple. For 'cuff', picture a shirt or cuff link. For the King of Clubs, picture the item to be associated as sitting on a throne, being the 'king'. The same goes for the Queen of Hearts – be sure that in your pictures for 'king' and 'queen' you have something to distinguish one from the other. (Picturing 'queen' in a long flowing gown, and the 'king' in knee breeches would do it.) If you had to remember that the King of Clubs was the 19th card, you could picture a 'tub' (19) sitting on a throne, wearing a crown, and being a 'king'. Another idea, of course, would be to see a king wearing a tub instead of a crown. Either picture is a good one.

For the word 'hoof', it's best to picture a horseshoe; for 'hose', you can see either a garden hose, or ladies' hose; for 'hinge', picture the associated item being hinged. If you

wanted to remember that the Two of Spades was the 29th
card, you might see a gigantic door 'knob' (29) instead of the
'sun' (2S) shining in the sky with a tremendous brilliance.
For 'sum', picture a sheet of paper covered with numbers;
or an adding machine. For the word 'sore', I usually picture
the associated item with a large bandage, as if it had a
wound or sore. 'Sash' – picture a window sash. 'Steam' –
picture a radiator. For 'sing', you can picture a sheet of
music, or you can see the associated item singing. 'Date' –
picture the fruit, or a calendar. 'Dash' – picture the
associated item running the 100-yard dash. 'Dive' – picture
the item diving into a body of water. 'Deb' – is the
abbreviation of debutante. For 'dose' it is best to picture a
spoonful of medicine.

The few suggestions above are just that – suggestions.
You must decide which picture you will 'see' for each card
word, just as you did with the number words. After you've
decided, use that picture only. Use any picture that the word
brings to mind; but be sure that the mental picture for any
card word does not conflict with the mental picture of any
of your number pegs from 1 to 52.

You now have all you need to memorize a complete pack
of cards. Since each card is represented by an object, you
simply use the Peg system as if you were memorizing a list
of fifty-two objects! That's all there is to it. If the first card
is the Five of Spades, you might see a large tie (1) acting as
a *sail* on a boat; or, you're wearing a sailboat instead of a
tie. If the second card were the Eight of Diamonds, you
could see Noah (2) *diving* into the water. Third card – Two of
Spades – see your ma (3) in the sky instead of the *sun*.
Fourth card – Queen of Diamonds – see a bottle of rye (4)
sleeping and dreaming; or, you are dreaming of a bottle of
rye. Fifth card – Three of Clubs – see a gigantic *comb*
walking the beat like a *cop* (law – 5), or a policeman is
arresting a comb, and so on.

When you are demonstrating this for your friend, have the
peg word for 1 in your mind before he starts calling the
cards. As soon as you hear the first one, associate the card

word for that particular card with the peg word 'tie'. Then immediately get the peg word for 2 in your mind, etc. When you've memorized the entire pack in this fashion, call the cards off in order, from one to fifty-two! You can have your friend call any number and you tell him the card at that position, or, have him call any card and you tell him at which number it is in the pack.

Of course, you don't have to memorize the entire pack to impress your friends. If you wish to present a faster demonstration, you can remember half the pack. This is just as effective, because it is just about impossible for anyone with an untrained memory to remember twenty-six cards, in and out of order.

However, if it is a fast demonstration you want, the one that follows is the fastest, most impressive, and yet the easiest of them all! This is called the 'missing card' stunt. You have anyone remove, say, five or six cards from a complete pack, and have him put them in a pocket. Now, let your friend call the remaining cards to you at a fairly rapid pace. After he has called all of them, you tell him the names of the five or six *missing* cards!

I told you that this was easy to accomplish, and it is. Here is all you have to do: as soon as a card is called, transpose it to the representative card peg word, and then – *mutilate that object* in some way! That's it! Let me explain. Assume that the Four of Hearts is called – just 'see' a picture of a *hare* with no ears. If the Five of Diamonds is called, see a *doll* with an arm or leg missing. If you hear the King of Diamonds, see a spilled *drink*. That's all you have to do. Don't linger over your associations, just see the picture for the merest fraction of a second, and you're ready for the next card.

This can be done quickly because you are cutting out one mental callisthenic, so to speak. You're not using your number pegs at all. Of course, the speed with which the cards can be called is just a matter of practice. I can assure you that after a while, you will practically 'see' the picture in your mind, before your friend is through naming the card!

Now – after all the cards have been called, go over the words for the cards in your mind. The best way to do this is to go from Ace to King of one suit at a time. When you come to an object that is *not* mutilated or broken in any way, that *must* be one of the missing cards! For example, you start down your list of words for the Club cards: cat – you had pictured the cat without a tail. Can – you had seen a tin can that was crushed. Comb – you had pictured a comb with all its teeth missing or broken. Core – you do not recall anything wrong with the core, therefore, the Four of Clubs is one of the missing cards. The *un*mutilated words will stand out in your mind like a sore thumb as soon as you come to them. You need only try it once, to be convinced.

I suggest that you always use the same suit order when going over your card words mentally. It doesn't matter which order you use, as long as you can remember it easily. I use Clubs, Hearts, Spades and Diamonds because it's easy to remember. Just think of the word – *CH*a*Se*D. If you wanted to use Hearts, Spades, Diamonds and Clubs order, you could remember that, by thinking of the phrase – *Hi*S De*C*k.

Incidentally, if you wanted to demonstrate your Bridge playing technique, you could do the missing card stunt with thirteen missing cards. The number of cards taken from the pack before the pack is called to you doesn't make any difference. You could even have half the pack called, and then name all the cards in the other half!

After my own performances, I think that the thing my audiences talk about the most, except perhaps names and faces, are the card demonstrations that I do. They are very impressive to most people, whether or not they play cards.

I'm sure that most of you have read this far without actually learning the card words. Now that you see the things you can do with them, I hope you *will* learn them. By the way, do any of you see how you can apply the missing card idea to games like Gin Rummy, Bridge, Pinochle, Casino, or for that matter, to any game where it is to your advantage to know which cards have or haven't been played? I will leave that to you.

In a later chapter, you will find some more stunts and ideas with cards. However, one more thought before I close this chapter – if you wanted to remember a pack of cards *in order* only, you could do it quickly by using the Link method alone! You would simply link the card pegs to each other as they were called. Of course, you wouldn't know them out of sequence with this method.

I keep telling you to have the cards called off to you; but it's just as good to *look* at the cards to remember them. It just adds a little to the effect upon your spectators, if you do not look at them.

After going over the card words mentally, a few times, you can use a pack of cards to help you practise. Shuffle the pack, turn the cards face up, one at a time, calling out or thinking of the peg word for each one. When you can go through the entire pack at a fairly brisk pace without hesitating, *then* you know your card words.

And when you do, would you try your new-found ability on Test 4 in Chapter 3? I think you will be pleased at the difference in your scores.

11 It pays to remember long digit numbers

The memory is a treasurer to whom we must give funds, if we are to draw the assistance we need. *Rowe*

Once, during my performance at the Concord Hotel in upstate New York, a 'friend' in the audience asked me to memorize the number 414,233,442,475,059,125. I did, of course, using my systems. The reason I mention this now is because I had forgotten the little stunt I used as a child. I would boast to my friends of what a marvellous memory I had, and ask one of the boys (a stooge, of course) to call out a long digit number. He would then proceed to call out the subway stops of the New York Sixth Avenue Subway. We all knew these stops, and it would have been quite obvious if he had said '4', then '14', and then '23', and so on. However, hearing the numbers in groups of three made them unrecognizable to the uninitiated.

In those days the Sixth Ave express stopped at West 4th Street, then 14th Street, 23rd Street, 34th Street, 42nd Street, 47th and 50th Streets, 59th Street, 125th Street, etc. I would simply call off these stops and leave my pals exclaiming over my prodigious memory. This all proves that numbers *can* be remembered if they are made to represent or mean something to us. I have helped you to do just that by utilizing the Peg system. Now, any number, whether it represents subway stops or not, can be made to mean something to you. And, in my personal opinion, that is the *only* way to memorize and retain a number. Yes, I've heard of the few rare cases of people who could memorize numbers instantly. I've heard of one person who could remember and retain long numbers as they were flashed before his eyes. (I wish I could do it!) These people don't know *how* they remember, they just do. Unfortunately, these are the few exceptions that strengthen my belief.

How would you go about memorizing the number 522641637527? Here is the way a memory expert of the nineteenth century did it. He told his students to separate the number into four sections of three digits each: 522 641 637 527. Now, I quote:

bring the first and fourth groups into relation, and you see at once that the fourth group is larger than the first by only five. Bringing the second group into relation with the third section, we find they differ only by four. Again, the third group is larger than the fourth by 100 and by 10, that is 527 becomes 637, the seven alone remaining steadfast. Beginning with the fourth group and passing to the third, we have the fourth group with 110 added. The second group is the third group with only four added, and the first group is the fourth group with only five subtracted.

This system, without any modification, is also taught by some modern memory experts. When I first heard of the above method of memorizing numbers, I felt that one would have to have a trained memory in the first place, just to remember the instructions! As far as retaining the number is concerned – well, I think it highly improbable that you would retain it for any length of time – *if* you memorized it at all. There were no ridiculous pictures or associations made to remind you of it. I believe, however, that I see the point that these memory experts were probably driving at. If you do try to follow their instructions, you must concentrate on the number. This, of course, is half the battle won. Any method that forces the student to be interested in, and to observe the number, and to concentrate on it, must meet with some success. It's just that it is too much like swatting a fly with a sledge hammer; the means are almost too burdensome to justify the end.

The Peg system of memorizing long digit numbers is actually a combination of the Peg and the Link methods. It forces you to concentrate on the number; it is easy to do –

and the retentiveness is amazing! If you have learned the list of peg words from 1 to 100 this should be easy for you. If you haven't learned them yet, this will make you want to do so. For the time being, you can make up the words as you go along. I'll use the same number as used above to explain the method.

First, let's break the number down into two-digit numbers. 52 26 41 63 75 27. Now, each of these two-digit numbers should represent or suggest a peg word to you:

52	26	41	63	75	27
lion	notch	rod	chum	coal	neck

All you have to do is to make a link of the six peg words! Or, any words you happen to be using. Picture a *lion* with a large *notch* in him. Picture yourself whittling notches into a gigantic curtain *rod*. See yourself throwing your arms around the rod as if it were your *chum*, or, your chum is being used for a curtain rod. Picture yourself embracing a large piece of *coal* as if it were your chum; and, finally, see yourself or anyone with his *neck* made of coal.

You should be able to make this link in about thirty seconds. After you've made it, go over it once or twice in your mind to see if you've memorized it. In repeating the number, all you do is transpose your peg words back to numbers. You'll know the number now, forwards *and* backwards! In actual practice, you should form your peg words and link them as you move your eyes from left to right across the number.

There you have it! You merely linked six objects to memorize twelve digits, and you will retain them for as long as you desire. If you have tried this while I explained it, and if you remember the number, you should feel proud of yourself. I say this because, according to some of our intelligence quotient tests, the average adult should remember a *six*-digit number forwards and backwards, after hearing or seeing it once. The superior adult should do the same with an eight-digit number. You've just accomplished it with a twelve-digit number, and there is no limit to the retentiveness.

Don't let anyone talk you out of it, either, by telling you 'not fair' because you used a 'system'. Those that do say this are surely envious of you because they can't do it, system or not. There are always those that scream, 'It's unnatural to remember with a system; you have to do it by normal memory.' Well, who's to say that this method is unnatural? It is surely more natural to remember than to forget. And, by using any of my systems you're simply *aiding your true memory*! As I explained earlier, anything that anyone

remembers must be associated to something they already know and remember. People do it all the time, sometimes consciously, sometimes without realizing it – all we are doing is systemizing it. There's a 'method' to our madness! Those that say memory systems are unnatural really mean, I think, that *they* don't know about them, or how to use them.

Now that I've defended your recently acquired facility to remember, let's go a step further. If you've grasped the idea, which I'm sure you have, why not use your imagination and make it even easier. If you like, you can link only four words in order to memorize a twelve-digit number. Just make up words to fit *three* of the digits at a time, and link those. For example, you could picture a bolt of *linen* (522) riding a *chariot* (641) which is dragging a *shoe*mak*er* (637 – the last consonant sound is disregarded since you know that the word represents only three digits) who is very *lank*y (527).

Here is another example:

$\frac{994}{\text{paper}}$	$\frac{614}{\text{ashtray}}$	$\frac{757}{\text{clock}}$	$\frac{954}{\text{bowler}}$

If a long digit number that you wish to remember falls into line for words that fit *four* digits at a time – why not use them! In that way you can sometimes memorize and retain a *twenty*-digit number by linking only five words:

42109483521461279071

Doesn't that number look formidable? It certainly does! But look at it now:

$\frac{4210}{\text{rents}}$	$\frac{9483}{\text{perfume}}$	$\frac{5214}{\text{launder}}$	$\frac{6127}{\text{cheating}}$	$\frac{9071}{\text{basket}}$

Link rents to perfume, perfume to launder, launder to cheating, cheating to basket – and you've memorized a twenty-digit number!

If, in your particular business, you find it necessary to memorize long numbers very often, you'll soon use the first word that pops into your mind to fit either the first two, three or four digits. There is no rule that says you must use words to fit the same number of digits in any long digit number. To memorize the number quickly, you use any words at all – usually you will have time to think for a moment to find the best words for the number to be memorized. I have to leave this to your own imagination. However, until you've become proficient at it, I would suggest that you use the peg words for two digits at a time.

You can see now the importance of knowing the ten basic sounds of the phonetic alphabet thoroughly. If you haven't learned them yet, re-read the chapter on how to learn and practise them. If you are not sure of how to make ridiculous or illogical associations – re-read that chapter. If you *do* know the sounds, the peg words and how to make your associations, try your knowledge on Test 3, in Chapter 3, and *see* the progress you've made.

12 Some pegs for emergencies

The memory is always present; ready and anxious to help – if only we would ask it to do so more often. *Roger Broille*

Many times when I've been challenged to prove that anyone can remember by using something similar to the Peg system, I would use a method which taught the sceptic to memorize ten miscellaneous objects forwards and backwards, and in and out of order, in about five minutes. What I did was to put ten small items, in a row, on a table; items like a ring, a watch, a cigarette, a match book, a comb, etc. I then told the person that these ten objects were to represent the numbers from one to ten.

Now I taught him to associate the item I called to the object on the table which represented the number called. In other words, if I called 'typewriter' as 7, and the seventh item on the table was the ring, he would associate 'typewriter' to ring. Later on, when I asked if he remembered 7, he would count to the seventh object, the ring, which would remind him of the typewriter.

This usually convinced the sceptic that he could remember better than he thought he could, but he always wanted to know if he'd have to carry those ten items with him. Of course, if he memorized those ten things he would have had a list of ten pegs to which to associate any other ten objects. But, it is a bit difficult to memorize ten completely unassociated items to use for a peg list; and, in this case, would hardly be worth the trouble.

However, as I mention elsewhere in the book, it was Simonides who first used the rooms of his house, and the furniture in the rooms as a peg list. And, this idea will work just as well today, except that it is a bit limited. Also there is too much sameness in pieces of furniture to make a useful list. There is the possibility of becoming confused, and it would take time to know which *number* each piece represented.

There have been a great many ideas thought up on how to devise peg lists. I've heard of one man who used twenty-six women that he knew, whose names each began with a different letter of the alphabet. This gave him a list of twenty-six pegs. If he wanted to remember that, say, typewriter was 16, he would associate typewriter to *P*auline. This will work; but again – too much sameness; each peg must create a distinctly different picture in your mind if it is to work properly.

There are some ideas besides the phonetic alphabet which can be used just as well, except that they are limited in length. For instance, I have had occasion to need a few short peg lists to help me recall up to twenty or twenty-six items. Well, there are two methods that I've used quite often. The first is to use the twenty-six letters of the alphabet. All you have to do is to make up a word for each letter which sounds like the letter itself. Look at this list:

A – ape
B – bean
C – sea
D – dean
E – eel
F – effort (or effervescent)
G – jean (or gee, command to horse)
H – ache
I – eye
J – jail
K – cake
L – elf
M – ham
N – hen
O – eau (water)
P – pea
Q – cute
R – hour (clock)

S – ass
T – tea
U – ewe
V – veal
W – Waterloo
X – eggs
Y – wine
Z – zebra

If you go over this list once or twice, you'll have it.
Decide on a picture for each one, and use that all the time.
Now you have a list which will enable you to memorize up
to twenty-six objects. For 'B', I used 'bean' only because
'bee' would conflict with your basic peg word for 9. Of
course, there are other words that can fit for some letters,
and you can use any that you like. Just be sure that they do
not conflict with your basic list of pegs. The words listed
above are the ones that I use.

Incidentally, if you made a link from zebra to ape, you
would be able to recite the alphabet backwards, which is
quite a feat in itself. If you want to, you can associate each
letter word to your regular peg word for that particular
number. In this way you would know the numerical position
of each letter immediately: ape to 'tie'; bean to 'Noah'; sea
to 'ma', and dean to 'rye', etc.

Another idea I use is to make a list of nouns, each of which
look like the number they represent. You can do this with
many numbers, and for those that you can't, you can make
up any picture to remind you of it. For 1, you might picture
a *pencil*, because a pencil standing upright looks like the
figure 1. For 2, you can picture a *swan*; a swan on a lake
is shaped something like the figure 2. I usually picture a
three-leaf *clover* for 3. A *table* or chair, or anything with
four legs can represent 4. For 5, you can see a five-pointed
star. A *yo-yo* on a string, with a little stretch of the
imagination, looks like a figure 6.

A *golf club* held upside down is similar in shape to 7. For
8, you could picture an *hour-glass*. For 9, I use a *tape
measure*. I mean the tape measures that are made of metal

and unroll from a round container. If you pull the tape out about six inches, the thing looks like a figure 9. A *bat* and *ball* pictured side by side can represent 10; the bat is the digit 1, and the ball is the zero. I picture *spaghetti* for 11; my original picture was of two pieces of raw spaghetti lying side by side, which looked like 11. For 12, you can think of 12 o'clock and picture a *clock*.

You can use either a white cat or walking under a *ladder* for 13. My original picture for 14 was a straight running river or stream to represent the 1, and a farm that looked like the figure 4 from the air. If you can create this picture in your mind – looking from an aeroplane and seeing this farm adjacent to the river, they would look like 14. You can then use either *farm* or river, or both, to represent the number.

I pictured myself stepping into an elevator and saying, 'Fifteenth floor, please', for 15. I now use *elevator* to represent the number. For 16, I pictured a road *sign* that said, 'Route 16'.

I have used this list for years to help me memorize sixteen objects. There is no reason for you to stop at sixteen. You can use the same idea to bring the list up to twenty, or

Some pegs for emergencies   87

higher if you like. No thought or picture is too far-fetched if it suggests a certain number to you, then it will serve the purpose. Just get your imagination working.

Anyway, here is the list as I've used it, up to 16:

1 – pencil	9 – tape measure
2 – swan	10 – bat and/or ball
3 – clover	11 – spaghetti
4 – table	12 – clock
5 – star	13 – white cat (or ladder)
6 – yo-yo	14 – farm (or river)
7 – golf club	15 – elevator
8 – hour-glass	16 – sign

There are other ideas which I could list; but I won't. If you need any more lists, you can use your imagination to help you form them. I'm sure you realize that the phonetic alphabet, and the letter or number equivalent method taught in this book, is far superior to any of the methods mentioned in this chapter. Your basic list of peg words could be brought up to a thousand, or over, if you wanted to, and the beauty of it is that as soon as you heard one of them, the sounds in the word would tell you immediately which number it represented. The phonetic alphabet makes it possible for peg words to be at your fingertips for any number; you don't have to make them up and remember them in advance, either, you can make them up when, or as, you need them.

The two ideas I've suggested to you here, however, can be useful if you need a short list quickly, or, if you want to use one of them in conjunction with your basic peg words. The latter idea can be used for some amazing memory feats, as you will learn in a later chapter.

Before closing this chapter, I just want to remind you again that none of these ideas are too far-fetched. Any one of them will work for you if you make up your mind to use them. The two listed here are, as far as I'm concerned, the best of the lot; but *any* list of words that you happen to know in sequence can serve as a peg list. I know one man who uses his own body for this purpose. From head down, he uses hair, forehead, eyes, nose, mouth, chin, neck, chest, all the way down to toe for his peg list. So, if an object to be remembered were 3, he would associate it to 'eyes', if it were 7, he would associate it to 'neck', and so on.

Some of the old-time memory experts who performed in vaudeville would use the theatre itself to help them do the stunt of memorizing objects called by the audience. They might have used the stage for 1, the footlights for 2, the orchestra for 3, stalls for 4, balcony for 5, etc. Anything in the theatre was utilized; the draperies, chandeliers, exit signs, men's room, ladies' room, etc.

And, of course, one of the most common (and most limited) peg lists is the one which uses words that sound like the numbers. Such as gun for one, shoe for two, tree for three, door for four, and so on, up to hen for ten, which is about as far as you can go.

Well, I guess my main reason for telling you about all these other ideas for word lists was to show off the effectiveness of the phonetic alphabet. As far as I know, there is no other idea that approaches it for its unlimited qualities and for its versatility.

In the next chapter you will see how either one of the lists you learned here, or parts of them, can be used in conjunction with the phonetic alphabet.

13 It pays to remember dates

'What day is today?'
'You've got me, I don't know what day it is.'
'Well, why don't you look at that newspaper you have in your pocket – that should tell us.'
'Oh, no, that won't do us any good; it's yesterday's paper!'

Although all of us *can* tell what day today is by looking at yesterday's paper – how many of you can tell quickly, or slowly, for that matter, the day of the week that any date this year will fall on? Not many, I'm sure. If you feel that having this information at your fingertips, with hardly any effort, is worth while – then read on. There are, of course, many different methods for calculating the day of the week for any given date, not the least of which is counting on your fingers.

Some of the systems are so involved that it seems much simpler to take the time to find a calendar, and get your information there. On the other hand, there are ways of actually knowing the day of the week for *any* date in the twentieth century! This doesn't seem to me to have any particular practical value; although it may have for some of you. Used as a memory stunt, however, it is quite impressive.

I intend to teach you how to do that in this chapter, but first, for practical use, I have come across a very simple way to find the day of the week for any date of the current year. This idea is so easy that most of you will wonder why you didn't think of it yourselves. This is it for the year 1957;

All you have to do is memorize this twelve-digit number – 633752741631 – the way you've been taught to do. You can break the digits down into your peg words and link them, or

make up words to take in more than two digits at a time.
For example, you can remember this number by making a
link of these four words, chum, mug, linger and dishmat.
Once you have memorized the number you can tell the day
of the week for any date of the year 1957! Each digit in the
number represents the first Sunday of the month for one of
the twelve months! The first Sunday in January falls on
6 January; the first Sunday in February falls on 3 February;
the first Sunday in March is 3 March; 7 April is the first
Sunday in April; 5 May is the first Sunday in May, and so on.

All right, so now you know the day of the month upon
which the first Sunday falls for each month. How can this
help you to know the day of the week for any date of the
current year? Simple! You wish to know the day of the
week for 22 August 1957 – you know that the first Sunday
of August is the 4th of the month. Knowing this, your
calculations are elementary. If the 4th is a Sunday, then the
next Sunday is the 11th and the following Sunday the 18th.
The 18th is a Sunday, so the 19th is Monday, the 20th is
Tuesday, the 21st is Wednesday, and, of course, 22 August
is a Thursday!

Do you want to know the day of the week on which
Christmas falls this year (1957)? Well, thanks to the
twelve-digit number, you know that the first Sunday of
December is the 1st of the month. Therefore the 8th must
be a Sunday, the 15th is a Sunday, and the 22nd is a Sunday.
If 22 December is a Sunday, then the 23rd is Monday, the
24th is Tuesday, and 25 December (Christmas) must fall
on *Wednesday* this year!

Here is the way my mind actually works when I want the
day of the week for any date this year: I use the words
chum, mug, linger and dishmat to remember the twelve
digits. I know that the word 'chum' gives me the first
Sunday of the month for January and February. The word
'mug' tells me the first Sunday of March and April. 'Linger'
gives me the same information for May, June, July and
August, and I know that 'dishmat' represents September,
October, November and December.

Now, if I wanted to know the day of the week for, say, 9 November 1957 – I immediately think of 'dishmat'. I know that the third consonant sound of this word represents the first Sunday of November. The first Sunday is the 3rd, therefore 10 November is also a Sunday; and, if the 10th is a Sunday, 9 November must be a *Saturday*.

If, in your particular business, it would be a help if you knew the day of the week for the present year *and* the following year – get a hold of next year's calendar, and memorize the twelve digits for that year by making up a link of four or five words. You could do this for as many years as you want to, but I don't believe it's practical for more than two years. However, the memory feat that follows is also a practical method of knowing the day of the week for any date in the twentieth century.

As a stunt, you would tell your friends that you've memorized all the calendars of the twentieth century. To prove it, ask them to call out any date; a date of which they themselves know the day of the week. This is necessary, of course, so that they can check your answer. Most people remember the day of the week of their wedding, graduation or other important anniversary. When the date is called, you almost immediately tell them the day of the week for that particular date!

To accomplish this you must know two things *besides* the month, day and year: a certain number for the year, which I will refer to as the 'year key', and a certain number for the month, which I'll call the 'month key'.

Perhaps if I explained the method and procedure before going into the technicalities you would find it easier to understand. This is it: let's assume that you want to know the day of the week for 27 March 1913. Let's also assume that you know the 'year key' for 1913 is 2, and that the 'month key' for March is 4. You would add these two keys, arriving at 6. Now you add this number (6) to the day, in this particular case – 27 (27 March). This gives you a total of 33. The last step is to remove all the *sevens* from your total. Seven goes into 33 four times ($4 \times 7 = 28$); remove

28 from 33, which gives you a final total of 5. That is your day – the *fifth* day of the week is *Thursday*!

27 March 1913, did fall on a Thursday! Please don't consider this complicated; it isn't. Actually you will never have to add any numbers higher than seven. The keys for the years and the months are all either 0, 1, 2, 3, 4, 5, or 6. Sevens are always removed as soon as possible. If you had to add a 'year key' of 5 to a 'month key' of 6, you would arrive at 11; but immediately remove one seven, which leaves you with 4. The 4 is all you would have to keep working with. If the day that is given you is higher than seven, you remove all the sevens, i.e. the date is the 16th; remove the two sevens ($2 \times 7 = 14$) and use the remainder of 2 only. In the above example, you would simply add 4 to 2, which tells you that the day of the week is the sixth, or Friday.

I will give you a few more actual examples, after I acquaint you with the year and month keys, and my methods for remembering them.

These are the month keys, which will always remain the same:

January – 1	July – 0
February – 4	August – 3
March – 4	September – 6
April – 0	October – 1
May – 2	November – 4
June – 5	December – 6

I'll give you a memory aid for remembering each of these keys. The method that follows is one way, and I'll explain one other. You can use whichever you like best, or one which you think of yourself.

January is the *first* month of the year; therefore it is easy to recall that the key for January is 1.

February is a *cold* month, it usually has plenty of *snow*; both the words 'cold' and 'snow' have *four* letters, so the key for February is 4.

In March the *wind blows*. Both 'wind' and 'blow' have

four letters; which will help you to remember that the key for March is 4.

April is known for its *showers*. 'Showers' has seven letters; all the sevens must be removed $(7 - 7 = 0)$; so we know that the key for April is zero.

The key for May is 2. Do you recall the game we used to play when we were children, the one in which we would say, '*May* I take 2 giant steps?' Well, if you remember that phrase, you will recall that the key for May is 2. Or, you might think of 'May Day', or 'May Pole', consisting of *two* words.

'June Bride' is a common phrase; 'bride' has *five* letters, so you will remember that the key for June is 5.

For July, you could use this for a memory aid: Most people know that 4 July is a celebration of the signing of the American Declaration of Independence in 1776. Take the two sevens from the year 1776, leaving 1 and 6. One and six are seven; remove this seven, leaving 0. Or, 4 July is usually associated with fire crackers; the word 'cracker' has seven letters; remove the seven, leaving 0. The key for July is zero.

August is a *hot* month. The word 'hot' has three letters; the key for August is 3.

September is the month during which the *leaves* start turning brown. 'Leaves' has six letters; the key for September is 6.

Octo means eight, remove the seven $(8 - 7 = 1)$ leaving one. The key for October is 1.

November is the 11th month of the year, remove seven, leaving four, so the key for November is 4.

Finally, the big holiday in December is Christmas. Christmas is the anniversary of the birth of Christ. 'Christ' has six letters, so we know that 6 is the key for December.

Although some of the above may seem a bit far-fetched, they *will* help you remember the keys. Another way would be to form a *substitute word* for each month (the system of substitute words will be explained thoroughly in the following chapter), and associate that to the peg word that represents its key number. For zero, use any word that contains the s or z sound only; 'zoo' is good, because it is easy to picture.

Here are some suggestions as to substitute words for all twelve months:

January – Jan. – Abbreviation of 'janitor'. Associate janitor to 'tie'.

February – Fib or fob. Associate any of these to 'rye'.

March – See the object associated (rye) marching.

April – Ape.

May – Use a person whose name is May, or picture a Maypole.

June – Picture a June Bride.

July – Jewel.

August – Gust of wind. Picture 'ma' being blown about by a gust of wind.

September – Sceptre or sipped.

October – Octopus or oboe.

November – Ember, new member.

December – Decimal, deceased or descend.

You can use either one of the two methods, or one that you make up yourself.

Now we come to the year keys. I'll give you all the keys for the years 1900 to 1987. All the years that have 1 for a key are listed together; the years with 2 are listed together, and so on.

I would suggest the use of another peg list to help you remember these keys. All you actually need is six words, representing the numbers 1 to 6, which will not conflict with your basic peg list. You can use any of the lists that I suggested in the previous chapter; the alphabet idea; ape, bean, sea, etc., or pencil, swan, clover, table, star, yo-yo, etc. For zero, use 'zoo' or 'sue'.

Since every year listed begins with 19, you don't have to try to remember that. Just associate the peg word for the last two digits of the year to the word that you are using to represent the key numbers.

For instance, the key for 1941 is 2. Associate 'rod' (41) to either 'swan' or 'bean', according to the list you're using. Make your associations for all of them. Go over them a few times and, before you know it, you'll have memorized them all.

1900	1901	1902	1903
1906	1907	1913	1908
1917	1912	1919	1914
1923	1918	1924	1925
1928	1929	1930	1931
1934	1935	1941	1936
1945 – 0	1940 – 1	1947 – 2	1942 – 3
1951	1946	1952	1953
1956	1957	1958	1959
1962	1963	1969	1964
1973	1968	1975	1970
1979	1974	1980	1981
1984	1985	1986	1987

1909	1904	1905
1915	1910	1911
1920	1921	1916
1926	1927	1922
1937	1932	1933
1943 – 4	1938 – 5	1939 – 6
1948	1949	1944
1954	1955	1950
1965	1960	1961
1971	1966	1967
1976	1977	1972
1982	1983	1978

You now have all the information necessary to do the calendar stunt, except for one thing. If it is a *leap year* and the date you are interested in is for either January or February – then the day of the week will be one day *earlier* than what your calculations tell you. For example – if you wanted to find the day of the week for 15 February 1944: the key for 1944 is 6. Add this to the key for February, which is 4, to get a total of 10. Remove the seven, leaving 3. Add the 3 to the day minus the sevens (15th day minus 14), which is 3 plus one, giving you a final total of 4. Four would ordinarily represent Wednesday, but in this case, you know that it is actually one day earlier, or Tuesday.

Remember that you do this only for January and February of a leap year. You can tell if a year is a leap year by dividing four into the last two digits. If four goes in evenly, with no remainder, then it is a leap year. (1944 – 4 into 44 is 11, no remainder.) The year 1900 is *not* a leap year.

Two more examples of the system:

        2 June 1923 – 0 plus 5 is 5
                      5 plus 2 is 7
                      7 minus 7 is 0
                      0 is Saturday.
    29 January 1937 – 4 plus 1 is 5
                      5 plus 29 is 34
                      34 minus 28 (4 × 7) is 6
                      6 is Friday.

See if you can find the day of the week for the following dates: 9 September 1906, 18 January 1916 (leap year), 20 August 1974, 12 March 1931 and 25 December 1921.

I don't intend to tell you that this system is easy to learn to do quickly; it does take some time and study, but, as I'm sure most of you know – nothing worth while comes too easily.

By the way, if you like this idea better than the one at the beginning of this chapter, and would like to use it for practical purposes – you could remember the 'year keys' of only the years you're interested in. That might be the previous year, the present year and the following year. With that, and your 'month keys', you would be able to know the day of the week for any date within those three years.

14 It pays to remember foreign language vocabulary and abstract information

The more intelligible a thing is, the more easily it is retained in the memory, and contrariwise, the less intelligible it is, the more easily we forget it. *Benedict Spinoza*

You may not think that the above quote shows any particular brilliance on the part of Mr Spinoza. You may feel, 'Of course, anyone knows that if something is intelligible, or makes sense, it is easier to remember.' Well, that's true, it is an obvious thought, but it took Mr Spinoza to say it, or put it down on paper just that way, as far back as the seventeenth century.

I'm making a fuss about this particular quote because it tells you in one sentence what this entire book is about. Almost all the systems in the book are basically that – they help make unintelligible things intelligible. One example, of course, is the Peg system; numbers by themselves are usually unintelligible, but the use of the Peg system makes them mean something to you.

Perhaps the best example is in trying to memorize foreign language vocabulary. A word in a foreign language is nothing but a conglomeration of sounds to anyone who is not familiar with the language. That's why they're so difficult to remember.

To make them easier to remember you will use the system of SUBSTITUTE WORDS. Substitute words or thoughts are used whenever you want to remember anything that is abstract, intangible or unintelligible; something that makes no sense to you can't be pictured, yet must be remembered. Be sure you read this chapter carefully, because substitute words will also help you to remember names.

Making up a substitute word is simply this: upon coming

across a word that means nothing to you, that is intangible and unintelligible, you merely find a word, phrase or thought that sounds as close to it as possible, and that *is* tangible and *can* be pictured in your mind.

Any word you may have to remember, foreign language or otherwise, that is meaningless, can be made to mean something to you by utilizing a substitute word or thought. Years ago I was a tropical fish hobbyist for a while, and I was trying to learn the technical names of the fish fins. Since I couldn't picture their names at that time, I used substitute words to remember them.

For example: the tail fin of a fish is called the *caudal* fin. In order to remember this, I made a picture of a fish with a long *cord* instead of a tail fin. The picture of a cord was enough to help me recall the word 'caudal'. The fin on the back of the fish is known as the *dorsal* fin. The first thought that came to my mind when I heard 'dorsal' was Tommy Dorsey (dorsal-Dorsey). I automatically associated Tommy Dorsey with a trombone. So, I simply made a picture in my mind of a man playing a trombone on the fish's back!

This may sound like a long procedure to you; it isn't. The association from 'dorsal' to Tommy Dorsey to trombone to the actual forming of the picture is the work of the merest fraction of a second. The thing for you to keep in mind is that the thought or picture that comes to *you* when you hear any intangible word is the one to use. I used Dorsey for dorsal, but you, perhaps, would have thought of 'door-sill', which would have served the purpose just as well.

The Spanish word for 'bird' is 'pajaro' (pronounced pa-kar-ro). Can you think of a substitute word for it? It's easy, because the word almost sounds like 'parked car'. Parked car, of course, is something that is tangible and which you can picture in your mind. So – why not make a ridiculous or illogical association, as you've already learned, between 'parked car' and 'bird'? You might 'see' a parked car crammed full of birds, or a bird parking a car, etc.

The next time you try to recall the Spanish word for 'bird'

your ridiculous association will help you to recall that the word is 'pajaro'. The substitute word you select does not have to sound exactly like the foreign word you're trying to remember. For 'pajaro' you might have used *pa carry*ing *eau* (water), or *parks* in a *row*, either of which would have also helped you to remember the word. As long as you have the *main* part of the word in your picture, the incidentals, the rest of the word, will fall into place by true memory.

This is strictly an individual thing; there are some substitute thoughts I use that I couldn't possibly explain in words, but they do help me recall the foreign word. The words I use may be suitable for me, but not for you; you must use the substitute thoughts that *you* think of.

I am explaining this so thoroughly because it is one of the most useful things you will learn in this book, and I want you to understand just what I'm talking about. To remember a foreign word and its English meaning, associate the English meaning to your substitute word for the foreign word.

Let me give you some concrete examples of the system, using a few simple Spanish and French words:

'Ventana' means 'window' in Spanish. You might picture a girl (one you know) whose name is *Anna*, throwing a *vent* through a closed window. If you wanted to remember the French word for 'window', which is 'fenêtre', you might picture a window *eating* a *raw fan*, or a fan eating a raw window. Fan-ate-raw – fenêtre!

The Spanish word 'hermano' (pronounced air-mon-o) means 'brother'. Just picture your brother as an *airman*.

The Spanish word for 'room' is 'cuarto' (pronounced quart-o). Picture a room piled high with *quarters*.

'Vasa' means 'glass' in Spanish. See yourself drinking from a *vase* instead of a glass.

The word for 'bridge' in French is 'pont'. See yourself *punting* a football on or over a bridge.

'Pluma' means 'pen' in Spanish. See yourself writing with a gigantic *plume* instead of a pen; or, you're writing on a plume with a pen.

The word meaning 'father' in French is 'père'. Associate father to *pear* and you'll always remember it.

The sample associations given above are those that I might use; it is always best to make up your own pictures.

Try this method with any foreign language vocabulary, and you'll be able to memorize the words better and faster, and with more retentiveness than you ever could before. Apart from languages, this system can be used for anything you may be studying which entails remembering words that have no meaning to you at first. A medical student who has to memorize the names of the bones in the human body may have some trouble with femur, coccyx, patella, fibula, sacrum, etc. But if these were made into substitute words or thoughts like this: fee more – femur; rooster (cock) kicks or cock sics – coccyx; pay teller or pat Ella – patella; fib you lie – fibula; and, sack of rum – sacrum – then the student could link them to each other, or associate them to whatever it is they must be associated to.

A pharmaceutical student could picture someone pushing a large *bell down* over him while he *throws pine* trees from under it, to help him remember that atropine (I throw pine) comes from the belladonna (bell down) root or leaf.

I am actually making up these substitute words as I write; with a little thought you could find much better substitute words for them. You might want to picture a giver (donor) of a bell to remember belladonna, etc.

The point is that the substitute word or thought has meaning while the original word does not. Therefore you make it easier to remember by using the substitute word. You will get some more pointers and practice on this in the chapter on how to remember names.

So – I started this chapter with a quote by Benedict Spinoza, may I be presumptuous enough to end it with a quote of my own – 'Anything that is intangible, abstract or unintelligible can be remembered easily if a system is used whereby the unintelligible thing is *made* to be tangible, meaningful and intelligible.'

15 It pays to remember names and faces

Two men approached each other on the street with a look of recognition in their eyes. One said to the other, 'Now wait a minute, don't tell me, I know I know you, but I'm not sure of where we met. Let me see if I can think of your name. I've got it! We met in Blackpool two years ago.'
'No, I've never been to Blackpool.'
'Hold it, don't tell me – oh, yes, it was in Brighton that we met.'
'Sorry, I've never visited Brighton.'
'I've got it now! Leeds in 1953!'
'No, I was not in Leeds in 1953.'
'Well, I know we've met, where *do* I know you from?'
'Idiot! I'm your brother!'

'Oh, I know your face, but I just can't remember your name!'

Although I doubt if any of you are as bad as the fellow in the anecdote, how often have you been embarrassed because you had to say this? I'm sure it has happened to you many times. If I were to take a poll as to why most people want to take my memory course, I think it would show that at least 80 per cent want to because they can't seem able to remember names and faces.

Usually, of course, it is the name that has been forgotten, not the face. The reason for this is quite simple. You see, most of us are what we call 'eye-minded'. In other words, things that we *see* register upon our brains with much more emphasis than what we hear. You always see the face, but usually only *hear* the person's name. That's why most of us, time after time, have to say, 'I recognize your face, but I can't remember your name.'

Not only can this be embarrassing, but can sometimes

hurt in business, and ultimately cost you money. Some people try to avoid this embarrassment by trying to trick people into giving their names before they themselves realize that their name has been forgotten. This might work occasionally, but not usually, and it still pays to *remember* the names. I'm sure you have all heard the old story about the man who met a business acquaintance whose name he couldn't recall. He tried to avoid embarrassment by pretending he knew the name, but wasn't sure of the spelling; so he asked, 'How do you spell your name again?' The reply was, 'The only way it *can* be spelled, J-O-N-E-S!' You see, this trick didn't work in this particular case.

Another sneaky way of pretending you didn't forget the name of someone you should have remembered is this: merely ask the person what his name is. If he tells you his second name, you say, 'Oh, I wouldn't forget *that*, it's your first name I meant.' If the person tells you the first name first, you, of course, say that you knew *that*, but it was the second name you wanted. In this way, you get the person's full name, and it seems as if you only forgot *one* of the names. There is only one thing wrong with this little bit of hocus-pocus. If the person gives you his *full* name as soon as you ask for the name in the first place, you're out of luck.

Then there is the classic example of the fellow who always asked people whose name he had forgotten whether they spelled it with an e or an i. This was fine, until he tried it with Mrs Hill.

No, I'm afraid it still pays to remember the name, instead of resorting to trickery. Not only does it pay to remember it but, believe me, it's easier than resorting to subterfuge because it takes much less effort.

People have tried various systems and methods to help their memory for names. Some use the alphabet, or first initial method. That is to say, they make a tremendous effort to retain only the initial of the person's name. This is more wasted effort, since they usually forget the initial anyway; and even if they remember the initial, how can that tell them the person's name? If you address Mr Adler as Mr Armanjian, or vice versa, he isn't going to be pleased just because the name you called him has the same first letter as his own.

Although writing things down on paper can sometimes be helpful in remembering, it cannot be depended upon as far as memorizing names is concerned. In conjunction with a good system of association – perhaps, as I will explain later, but not by itself. If you were able to draw an exact replica of the person's face, this would be better, since you would then know which name belongs to which face. You'd have your two tangibles with which to make some sort of ridiculous association. But, unfortunately, most of us can't draw that well, and if we could, it wouldn't be so helpful that it would make up for the time it would take.

Some memory teachers will tell their students to keep a 'memory book', and write down the name of every person they want to remember. As I've said, this might help a little if used together with a good system of association, but not otherwise. It might help some, of course, if you wanted to run down the list of names each time you meet a person, with the hope that the name will come to mind when you see it written in your book. If it did, I don't think you would feed the ego of the person whose name you 'fished' out of a book instead of out of your memory.

It isn't necessary, I'm sure, for me to tell you how important it is to remember names and faces. Yet, here is one of the most common memory complaints of modern times: 'I just can't remember names!' Our way of life today makes it almost unavoidable to meet many new people every day. You meet people continually, people you want to remember, and people that you do not think are important enough to bother remembering until you meet them again. Then when it is too late, you realize that you should have tried to remember.

Would it not be an asset for any salesman to remember the names of his customers? Or for a doctor to remember the names of his patients; a lawyer, his clients, etc.? Of

course it would. Everybody wants to be able to remember
names and faces, but many times an important sale is nipped
in the bud, money is lost, someone is caused to be
embarrassed or a reputation is stained, because someone
forgot an important person's name. Yet, even as far back as
early Greek and Roman civilization, Cicero remembered
the names of thousands of his villagers and soldiers, by
using a memory system.

There is a young lady that I've heard of, who is the hat
check girl in a popular New York night club. She has gained
a reputation, because she never issues a check for your hat
or coat. She simply remembers which hat or which coat
belongs to whom. It is said that she never yet has given
anyone the wrong article. This may not seem so important
to you, since it would be just as easy to do it with hat or
coat checks, the way all cloakroom attendants do it. But this
young lady has made herself into sort of an attraction at this
night club, and her sizeable tips prove it. Of course, this is
not exactly remembering names and faces, since she doesn't
remember the name, but it is similar enough. She must
associate the hat or coat, or both, to the person's face.

I've been told that the bellboy of a large hotel down south
has gained a similar reputation. Whenever someone checks
into the hotel who has been there even once before, this
bellboy addresses them by name. The last I heard, he is well
on his way to saving enough money out of his tips to buy
the hotel.

This should prove to you, if proof were necessary, that
people love to be remembered, they even pay for it. This
particular hat check girl and bellboy surely made more
money than the others who worked at the same jobs.

A person's name is his most prized possession, and there
is nothing more pleasing to him than hearing his own name
or having it remembered by others.

Some of my students and myself have remembered as
many as three hundred names and faces at *one* meeting and
you can do it too!

Before getting into the actual systems and methods for

remembering names and faces, I'd like to show you how you can improve your memory for them by at least 25 per cent to 50 per cent *without* the systems! Read the next few paragraphs very carefully.

The main reason that most people forget a name is because *they never remembered it in the first place*! I'll take that a step further, and say that they never even *heard* the name in the first place. How often have you been introduced to someone new, something like this: 'Mr Reader, meet Mr Stra—ph—is'? All you hear is a mumbled sound instead of the name. Possibly because the person who is doing the introducing doesn't remember the name himself. So, he resorts to double-talk. You, on the other hand, probably feel that you will never meet this person again, so you say, 'Nice to meet you', and you never bother to get the name right. You may even spend some time talking to the person and finally say good-bye, and still not hear the name properly.

The only thought most people will give to this situation is a self-questioning, 'What was that person's name? That nice gentleman I spoke to the other day?' When no answer is forthcoming, the entire thing is shrugged off with an, 'Oh, well', and that's that!

This is how people find themselves talking to others, and addressing them as Buddy, Old Pal, Fella', Sweetheart, Honey – anything you can think of to keep from finding it necessary to use the person's name, while you squirm with embarrassment because you don't *know* the name. Oliver Herford put it this way, when he gave his definition of the word 'darling': 'The popular form of address in speaking to a person of the opposite sex whose name you cannot at the moment recall.'

Here, then, is your first rule for remembering names: Be Sure You Hear The Name In The First Place! As I said before, you see the face, so the odds are you will recognize it when you see it again. You can only hear the name, so get it right. I have yet to hear anyone complain, 'I know your name, but I can't seem to remember your face.' It is

always the name that creates the problem. So, to repeat,
Be Sure You Hear The Name!

Don't let the fellow that's doing the introducing get away
with double-talk. If you haven't heard the name, if you're
not absolutely sure of it, ask him to repeat it. Sometimes,
even after hearing a name, you may not be sure of the
pronunciation; if that's the case, ask the person to spell it
for you. Or, try to spell it yourself; he'll correct you if you
spell it incorrectly, and he'll be flattered by your interest in
his name.

Incidentally, if you make a habit of trying to spell the
name of every new person you meet, you'll soon become
accustomed to the spelling of almost any kind of name.
You'll be surprised how many of them you'll spell correctly.
Eventually, you will be able to recognize how certain
sounds are spelled for certain nationalities. You'll learn
that the Italian language has no letter 'J', so the 'j' sound in
an Italian name is always spelled with a 'g'. The 'J' or the
soft 'G' sound, and sometimes the 'sh' sound in a Polish
name, is usually spelled 'cz', while the sound 'eye' is
sometimes spelled with the letters 'aj'. The 'ch' or 'tz'
sound in an Italian name is sometimes spelled with a double
'c'; the 'sh' sound in a German name, particularly at the
beginning of the name, is usually spelled 'sch', etc. Of
course, it doesn't *always* work – I recently came across a
name that sounded like 'Burke', but was spelled
'Bourque'. However, many of the people who have seen my
performance will vouch for the fact that I spell their names
correctly almost 85 per cent of the time. Or closely enough
to impress them, anyway. So, you see, it can be done. I
mention this because spelling a person's name correctly or
almost correctly will impress them almost as much as
remembering it.

If, after making sure of the spelling, you realize that the
name is the same or similar to that of a friend or relative of
yours, mention the fact. This all serves to impress the name
on your mind. If it is an odd name, one that you have never
heard before, say so. Don't feel shy, or as if you're

imposing when you do these things, because everybody is
flattered when you make a fuss over their names. Just as
they would be if you showed an interest in *any* of their
prized possessions, or in any of their particular interests.
This, I suppose, can be put down to human nature.

While talking to the person, repeat his name as often as
you can in the course of the conversation. Don't keep
jabbering it like an idiot, of course, just use it whenever you
feel it is apropos and necessary. I am not mentioning this
to be facetious. I've read some 'memory experts' '
instructions on this point, and they have given sample
conversations: 'Why, yes, Mr Greenpepper, I do sail to
Europe every season, Mr Greenpepper. And, oh, Mr
Greenpepper, don't you just adore Rome, Mr Greenpepper?
Mr Greenpepper, tell me this – etc. etc.,' and so on into the
night. This will not impress Mr Greenpepper, it will scare
him out of his wits.

No. Just use it, as I said, wherever and whenever you feel
it fits. *Do* use the name when you say goodbye or goodnight.
Don't just say something about hoping to meet again, say,
'Goodbye, *Mr Johnson*, I hope we'll meet again soon, etc.'
All this will etch the name more firmly and definitely into
your mind.

The only effort involved here as usual is just in doing this
the first few times. After that it will become habit and you
won't even realize that you are doing it. Make up your mind
to follow the hints suggested in the last few paragraphs.
Read them over, if you feel you're not sure of them.

For some people, all this in itself comprises a system for
remembering names. It is simply because by following the
above hints and suggestions you make names interesting,
you show interest, and in so doing you actually create
interest. And interest, as I've explained, is a large part of
memory.

All the above will help your memory for names and
faces by 25 per cent to 50 per cent, if you apply yourself;
but keep reading and I'll help you take care of the remaining
50 per cent to 75 per cent!

16 What's in a name?

This fellow was very proud of the way he could remember names by association, until he met Mrs Hummock. Mrs Hummock was quite heavy, and had a large stomach, so he decided to use 'stomach' as his association.
Three weeks later, he met the same lady, glanced at her stomach, and, feeling very pleased with himself, said, 'Good day, Mrs *Kelly*!'

Not very long ago I had the pleasure of performing for the executive club of a well-known department store in New York City. This was their annual dinner, and everyone was seated at tables in banquet style. The one demonstration in my performance that probably hits home for more people than any other is the one in which I remember everyone's name.

The way I usually do it is to introduce myself to all the guests as they arrive, or meet them while they're having dinner. I simply walk from table to table getting everyone's name (and becoming hungry). I'll meet all the people at one table, then the next, and the next, and so on, until I've met everyone in the room. I work as quickly or as slowly as time suggests. Many's the time that I've had to meet one hundred to two hundred people in fifteen minutes or less, without forgetting a single name! I give credit and praise to my methods and systems, of course, not to myself.

After I've met everyone, and after coffee and dessert, the show goes on. During the performance I ask everyone who has given me their name at any time during the evening to please rise at their seats. This most often consists of the entire audience. I then proceed to call the name of everyone standing; pointing to each particular person as I call his or her name. During the remainder of my lecture-demonstration, I allow anyone in the audience to interrupt me by shouting, 'What's my name?' and, of course, I immediately reply with the person's name.

The reason I am explaining all this is because I was amused at the explanation given by one of the department store executives, revealing how I did the 'trick' of remembering everyone's name at this particular affair. This, by the way, was not his idea of a joke, he was firmly convinced that this was how it was done.

The affair was held at the Capitol Hotel in New York City. The room we were in happened to have a circular balcony completely surrounding it. Following is the explanation given by the executive. He said:

Mr Lorayne has a photographer working with him. You know, one of those fellows who takes pictures at banquets and develops them in a few minutes so he can sell them to the people there and then. This photographer and Mr Lorayne both have tiny microphones and receiving sets hidden somewhere on their persons. The photographer is somewhere on the balcony, hidden, of course. There must be a hole up there, through which he can put the lens of his camera. Now, when everyone is seated, ready for dinner, he snaps a picture of the entire audience, which he develops and dries immediately.

When Mr Lorayne approaches a table and asks for the names, the photographer hears them too, thanks to the tiny microphones and receivers. He, the photographer, that is, has the picture in front of him; he spots the table that is giving the names (he can see through the hole), spots the particular person and listens to the name. He then writes that name on the picture, across the face of the person who gave it! He does this with every person in the room.

Now, you see how simple (*Author's note:* simple?) it is? When Mr Lorayne is performing, he always points to a person before he calls his or her name. The reason for the pointing is so that the photographer can spot that person on the picture, read the name, and quickly whisper it into his

microphone. Of course, Mr Lorayne hears it and calls the
person by name.

That's it. That was this gentleman's explanation of my
method. (Maybe it's not such a bad idea at that!) Of
course, he completely discarded all the other
demonstrations that I did during my performance. He
also forgot that many of the people change places after
dinner (most of the time I will meet the people in one
room, and do the show in another), and that after the show,
I spoke to the people away from the tables, in the lift, and
even in the street, and called them by name. Perhaps he
didn't forget; he may have thought that the photographer
was still whispering the names into his little microphone.
If that were the case, the photographer had a trained
memory.

I relate this incident only to show how difficult it is for
some people to believe that you actually can remember the
names and faces of an entire audience. They simply take the
path of least resistance and the negative attitude, and feel
that if *they* can't do it, no one else can; it's just impossible.
After reading my methods on how to remember names and
faces, I'm sure you will agree with me that it is not
impossible. On the contrary, it is much, much easier than
the method so emphatically believed by the department
store executive.

I would have been happy to send a copy of this book to
this particular gentleman, to prove it to him, too, only I
don't know his name; you see, I *forgot* where I put that
picture!

In previous chapters I've mentioned how important it is
to be interested in a person in order to remember his or her
name. If you were to be introduced to four hundred people
in one evening, and then perhaps meet these four hundred
people two or three more times, you would still forget most
of their names. If, however, you were to enter a room in
which there were four hundred celebrities, such as film stars,
you'd probably be able to call them all by their full names.
Not only that, but you could tell them at least one of the

films in which you have seen them perform. You'll agree, I'm sure, that this is because people are *interested* in celebrities and usually *want* to remember them. Well, I've already stressed the fact that being interested in and wanting to remember is half your battle won over a supposedly poor memory. Remember to use the rules that I gave you in the previous chapter.

Be sure you hear the person's name in the first place.

Spell it or have him spell it if you're not sure of it.

If there is any odd fact about the name, or if it is similar to a name you know, mention it.

Repeat the name as often as you can during the course of the conversation.

Use the name when you say goodnight or goodbye.

If you use these rules in conjunction with what I am about to teach you, you should never again forget a name or a face. To simplify the process, you will learn first what to do with the name, and then, how to associate the name to the face. Actually they go hand in hand; the name will conjure up the face, and the face will bring the name to mind.

All names can be separated into two categories: names that mean something, and names that have no meaning (to you) at all. Names like Cook, Brown, Coyne, Carpenter, Berlin, Storm, Shivers, Fox, Baker, King, Gold, Goodman, Glazer, and many others, all have a meaning. Names like Krakauer, Conti, Sullivan, Mooney, Littman, Carson, Linkfeld, Smolensky, Morano, Morgan, Resnick, Hecht, and so on, have no meaning at all to most of you. Of course, the lists are almost endless; these are just a few examples of each.

There are some names that fall into the 'no meaning' category, that do, however, suggest or create a picture in your mind. When you hear the name Sullivan you might think of or picture John L. Sullivan, the champion fighter. The name Lincoln would, of course, create or suggest a picture of the sixteenth U.S. president, Abraham Lincoln. Mr Jordan might suggest a picture of the River Jordan, while the name Di Maggio would make an American think of baseball. So, we arrive at *three* categories of names: those that actually have a meaning; those that have no meaning in themselves, but *do* suggest something to you; and finally, names that have no meaning and do not suggest or create a picture in your mind.

It is with the third category that you must use your imagination. You must, in order to remember the name, *make* it mean something to you. This is already so with the first two categories, so they are no particular problem. The names that have no meaning at all should present no problem either, if you have read the chapter on how to remember foreign language vocabulary. If you've read this chapter carefully, you know that you must utilize my system of 'substitute words or thoughts' in order to make the names mean something to you. No matter how strange the name sounds upon first hearing it, it can always be broken down to a substitute word or thought. Simply think of a word or phrase that sounds as much like the name as possible. If you were to meet a Mr Freedman, you might picture a *man* being *fried*. Fried man – Freedman. If the name were Freeman, you could picture a man holding or waving a Union Jack; he's free. You might want to picture a man escaping from prison; he's a free man. Remember, please, that whatever *you* decide on for your substitute word, phrase or thought, is the one to use. Ten people, given the same name to remember, may all use a different substitute word in order to remember it.

The name Fishter might make you picture a *fish stir*ring something, or stirring something with a fish. Fish stir – Fishter. Someone else may feel that picturing just a fish would be enough to recall the name. If you want to picture someone tearing a fish in half, or a fish tearing something in half, that would do it too. Fish tear – Fishter. You could picture yourself fishing and catching a *toe* instead of a fish. Fish toe – Fishter. Any one of these would suffice to help you remember the name.

It is not important to strain yourself to find a substitute word that sounds *exactly* like the name; or to use words for every part of the name. Remember what I told you some chapters ago: *If you remember the main, the incidentals will fall into place by true memory!* The very fact that you are thinking of and with the name, in this fashion, will help impress it on your mind. You have automatically become interested in the name merely by searching for a substitute word for it. That's why the anecdote that heads this chapter may be good for a laugh, but can't happen in actual practice.

Recently I had to remember the name Olczewsky, pronounced ol-chew-sky. I simply pictured an old man (I always picture a man with a long, flowing white beard to represent an *old* man) chewing vigorously, while he skied; old-chew-ski – Olczewsky. The name Conti might suggest soap (Conti Castile), or you might picture someone counting tea bags. Count tea – Conti. For the name Czarsty, you could picture a Russian Czar with a sty on his eye; the name Ettinger might suggest someone eating, or someone who has 'et' and injured himself, perhaps hurt a tooth, etc. Et injure – Ettinger.

It doesn't matter how silly you make it; more often than not, the sillier the better. I've often said that if I could explain on stage the silly associations that I've made to remember names, among other things, I'd have a very funny routine.

A name like D'Amico, pronounced Dam-ee-ko, is not too unusual a name. I've come across it a few times, and I've remembered it by picturing a woman seeing a dam overflow and screaming, 'Eek' and 'Oh'. Or picturing myself going towards an overflowing dam (the overflowing gets *action* into the picture) and saying, 'me go'. Dam eek oh, dam me go – D'Amico. This all sounds quite ridiculous. Good! The more ridiculous, the easier to tie the picture on to the face, as I will explain in a moment, and the easier to remember and retain the name.

After meeting a lot of new people, and using my systems, you will find that you'll have certain pictures or thoughts for names that you come across very often. I, for example,

always picture an ice-cream *cone* for the name Cohen or
Cohn. I see a black*smith*'s hammer for Smith or Schmidt.
Yes, I use the same picture for Smith and Schmidt; true
memory tells me the difference. You can prove this to
yourself only through your own experience. Here are some
other 'standards' that I employ:

The name Davis always makes me think of the Davis Cup
in tennis. So when I meet a Mr Davis, I always picture a
large loving cup. If the name were Davi*son*, I would picture
the large loving cup and a tiny one next to it; the large cup's
son. Sure, it's silly, but it works! Of course, the name Davis
may bring an entirely different picture to your mind. If it
does, use it. For the names ending with either 'itz' or
'witz', you can picture *itch* or brains (*wits*), i.e. Mr
Horowitz – you might picture yourself being horrified at
the sight of brains. Horror wits – Horowitz.

Many names end in either 'ly' or 'ton'. A lea is a meadow,
so I always get a meadow into my association to help me
recall 'ly'. 'Ton', of course, has a meaning. You might
picture a weight, a barbell or a dumb-bell to always
represent 'ton'. There are many names that either end or
begin with 'berg'; for these, I always use iceberg. The
suffix or prefix 'stein' always makes me picture a beer mug
or stein. I come across the suffix 'ler' quite often, as in the
name Brimler. 'Ler' sounds like *law* to me, and I always
picture a judge's gavel to represent law. You might decide to
picture a policeman or a jail or handcuffs to represent law;
that's O.K., just use the same picture for the ending 'ler'
each time. Eventually you will fall into a pattern with most
endings or entire names. This will make it easier and will cut
down on time if you have to meet and remember people
quickly.

The knowledge of a foreign language will sometimes help
in creating a picture or association. The name Baum means
'tree' in German. The name Berg means 'mountains'. If you
know this, you can use it in creating your substitute words
or thoughts. Just recently I met a Mr Zauber. When I
remarked that it was an odd name, he told me that in

German Zauber meant 'magician'. I had already pictured myself sawing a bear. Saw bear – Zauber. Either that or 'magician' would have helped me remember Mr Zauber.

I have a very close friend whose last name is Williams. His hobby happens to be playing billiards, at which he is exceptionally proficient. I have fallen into the habit of picturing someone shooting or playing billiards whenever I meet a Mr Williams. This works just as well as actually breaking down the name to *yams* (sweet potatoes) writing their *wills*. Will yams – Williams. The first time I met a Mr Wilson the first thought that came into my mind was the slogan for a whisky, 'Wilson, that's all'. Now, whenever I meet a Mr Wilson, I picture a bottle of whisky to help me remember his name.

So, as I pointed out, you will eventually fall into certain habits and use certain standards with particular names. Just keep in mind that there isn't a name that can't be made to mean something (to you) which will sound like the name itself and help in bringing it to mind, when necessary.

Although your best method of practice is to go ahead and use the system, here are some names which ordinarily are completely abstract; have no meaning at all. Why not see if you can create a substitute word, phrase or thought for each one.

Steinwurtzel	McCarthy
Brady	Gordon
Arcaro	Briskin
Moreida	Casselwitz
Kolodny	Hayduk
Platinger	Kolcyski
Hulnick	Pukczyva

If you had any trouble with any of the above names, here's the way I might have created substitute thoughts for them.

Steinwurtzel – a beer *stein worth sell*ing. Stein worth sell – Steinwurtzel.

McCarthy – I always picture the famous ventriloquial dummy, Charlie McCarthy, for this name.

Brady – You could picture a little girl's braids for this. If you want to get the entire name in your picture, see yourself braiding the lines of a large letter 'E'. Braid E – Brady.

Gordon – I always picture 'garden' for this name.

Arcaro – I usually see the famous American jockey of the same name. If you want to break the name down, see yourself carrying an 'O'. I carry O – Arcaro.

Briskin – You might want to picture someone *briskly* rubbing their *skin*. Brisk skin – Briskin.

Moreida – You could see yourself reading and calling for more and more books to read. Some of you may have thought of your mother (Maw) being a reader. More reader or Maw reader – Moreida.

Casselwitz – A *castle* completely stocked with brains (wits). You might see the brains actually oozing from all the windows. Castle wits – Casselwitz.

Kolodny – I would picture a large *knee* being all different *colours*. Coloured knee – Kolodny.

Hayduk – Ducks eating hay, or a hayloft or haystack full of ducks.

Platinger – Picturing a plate with a bandage would suffice. Plate injure – Platinger.

Kolcyski – Either a piece of *coal ski*ing in a *sit*ting position, or *call*ing your friend *Sid* to *ski* would do it. Or, it is too

cold to stand up and ski, so you *sit* and *ski*. Coal sit ski, call Sid ski, cold sit ski – Kolcyski.

Hulnick – you might see a little child being very happy because she has a *whole nickel*. A picture of a ship whose *hull* is made up of nickel or nickels would also do it. If you saw yourself *nick*ing a *hole* in something, you would still recall the name. Whole nickel, hull nickel, hole nick – Hulnick.

Pukczyva – This name is pronounced puck-shiv-va. I would see a hockey *puck shiver*ing with cold. Puck shiver – Pukczyva.

There you are. If you thought of entirely different pictures, don't worry about it. The point is that no matter how strange a name sounds, or how long it is, or how difficult to pronounce – you can always find a substitute word or thought for it. If the substitute word brings the name back to you, then that's the one to use, and in the next chapter I'll show you how to use them.

17 More about names and faces

Ruth was a sweet and lovely girl and had many boy friends, but her mother felt it was time she was married.

While reading a book on the meanings of names, Ruth said, 'Mother, it says here that Philip means "lover of horses", and James means "beloved". I wonder what George means?'

'I hope, my dear,' said Mother, 'that George means business!'

Now that you know how to make any name have meaning, by using a substitute word or thought, you have to know how to associate the name to the face in such a way as to remember both of them. Many memory systems teach the student to make a jinglet with the name; something like 'Mr Baker is a faker' or 'Mr Gold is old', or 'Mr Radcliffe had a mad tiff', or 'Mr Lillienkamp is a carnival tramp'.

This is fine, until you meet a Mr Nepomosimo or a Mr Smolensky. Even if you could create a rhyme with those names, what I never could quite grasp is how this would help you to remember the person's face, or rather, how *one* would bring the *other* to mind. No, I don't think that this jinglet system is of too great a help. In my opinion, the *only* way to remember a person's name is to associate that name *to* the person's face in some ridiculous way. And here's how to go about it.

Whenever you meet someone new, look at his face and try to find *one* outstanding feature. This could be anything; small eyes, large eyes, thick lips, thin lips, high forehead, low forehead, lines or creases on the forehead, long nose, broad nose, wide nostrils, narrow nostrils, large ears, small ears, ears that stand away from the head, dimples, clefts, warts, moustache, lines on the face, large chin, receding chin, type of hairline, jutting chin, small mouth, large mouth, teeth – just about anything.

You are to pick the one thing that seems most outstanding to you. It may not be *the* most outstanding feature; someone else may choose something entirely different. This isn't important; the thing that stands out to you is the thing that will be obvious and outstanding when you meet this person again. The point that is important is that as you're looking for this one outstanding feature you must pay *attention to* and be *interested in* the face as a whole. You're observing and etching this face into your memory.

When you have decided on the outstanding feature, you are ready to associate the name to *that* particular part of the face. For example, Mr Sachs has a very high forehead. You might 'see' millions of sacks falling from his forehead, or see his forehead as a sack *instead* of a forehead. You can see, of course, that you're to use the same laws and principles as you've been taught in the early chapters of the book. The most important principle being that you *must* actually see this picture in your mind's eye. Look at Mr Sachs's face, and 'see' those sacks falling from every part of his forehead. That's all there is to it! If Mr Robrum had a large nose, I would picture his nose as a bottle of *rum* and a *rob*ber stealing it!

Mr Horwick might have very bushy eyebrows, so I would see wicks in them, as in candles, and see a woman trying to take them because they are her wicks. Her wick – Horwick.

The original publisher of this book was Mr Frederick Fell. The moment I met Mr Fell I noticed a cleft in his chin. I simply saw things *fall*ing from this cleft, and that's all I needed to help me remember that his name was Mr Fell. Remember that, in these examples, I give the substitute thought and the outstanding feature that I personally think is best. The name 'Fell' could have meant 'feel' or the material 'felt' to you, and you could have associated that to any other feature on Mr Fell's face. The substitute word and the outstanding feature chosen is an individual thing; the things *you* choose are the right ones to use.

At first, some people may feel that it takes too long to find a substitute word for a person's name, and then associate it to his face. They think that it would be embarrassing to have people notice that they are staring at them. Please believe me, it does not take any time at all. After a minimum of practice you'll find that you've found a substitute word for the name (if it's necessary) and associated it to an outstanding feature on the person's face in less time than it takes to say 'Hello'. As in everything else, it's the very first effort that is the most difficult. Sure, it's easier to be lazy and just go on forgetting names, but, *try* my system and you'll soon agree that it is just as easy to remember them.

The best way to practise remembering names and faces is just to start doing it. However, to give you a bit of confidence, let's try this: I'm sure that before you started reading this book, most of you felt that you definitely couldn't remember and retain the names of fifteen people if you met them all at once. If you took the little test in Chapter 3, you probably proved it. Well, let me introduce you to the *pictures* of fifteen people right now, just to prove that you *can* do it, with the help of my systems. Of course it isn't as easy with pictures, since you see the faces in only one dimension, whereas ordinarily you see people in three dimensions. It may be a little difficult to find outstanding features of a face in a picture, but I'll try to help you with each one.

No. 1 is Mr Carpenter. This name is no problem because it already has meaning. The next step is to find an outstanding feature on Mr Carpenter's face. You might decide on his very small mouth. If you look closely, you'll see a sort of scar on his right cheek. Pick one of these (the one that's most obvious to you) and associate Carpenter to that. You might see a carpenter working on the small mouth (get the carpenter's tools into the picture) trying to make it larger; or, have the carpenter working on the scar, trying to repair it. Now, and most important, look at the picture of Mr Carpenter and actually *see* this picture, *see*

your association in your mind's eye for at least a split
second. You must make yourself '*see*' *this picture or you'll
forget the name*. Have you done that? If so, go to picture
No. 2.

No. 2 is the Mr Brimler we spoke about a while ago.
Notice the long dimples in his cheeks. Can you see the heavy
character lines from his nose to the corners of his mouth?
As in every face, there are many outstanding features that
can be used. I would use the dimples, and see them *brim* full
of judges' gavels. Remember, I use a gavel to represent law
or 'ler'. If you want to use policeman, jail or handcuffs, go
ahead. You might 'see' police brimming all over the dimples.
Whichever way you want to do it, is fine; but look at
Mr Brimler and *see* the picture you've decided on.

No. 3 is Miss Standish. I would select her 'bang' hair-do.
You could 'see' people *stand*ing on the bangs and scratching
themselves violently because they *itch*. Stand itch –
Standish. Of course, a *dish* standing would serve the same
purpose, but I like an association into which I can inject
some sort of action. Now look at Miss Standish and *see* the
picture you've decided on, in your mind's eye.

No. 4 is Mr Smolensky. Don't let the name scare you, it's
easy to find a substitute thought for it. I would see someone
ski-ing on Mr Smolensky's very broad nose, and taking
pictures (while ski-ing) with a *small* camera (lens). Small
lens ski – Smolensky. See how simple it is? I have chosen
Mr Smolensky's broad nose; you might think that the
receding chin is more obvious. Choose whichever *you* think
is most obvious, and *see* the picture of the skier taking
pictures with a small lens.

No. 5 is Mr Hecht. I would see his moustache being
hacked from his face with an axe. See the association
violently if you can. Violence and action make it easier to
recall. Hacked – Hecht. Be sure you *see* the picture.

No. 6 is Mrs Bjornsen, pronounced Byorn-son. The way
I would remember Mrs Bjornsen is to see a boy (son) being
born in the very wide part in her hair. You might think that
either her full cheeks, wide mouth, or dark eyes are more

1 MP CARPENTER

2 MR BRIMLER

3 MISS STANDISH

6 MRS BJORNSEN

7 MISS VAN NUYS

8 MR HAMPER

11 MR D'AMICO

12 MISS FORRESTER

13 MR PFEFFER

outstanding, if so, use those in your association. But look at Mrs Bjornsen and actually *see* the picture for a fraction of a second.

No. 7 is Miss Van Nuys. The first thing that I notice when I look at Miss Van Nuys are her bulging eyes. I would see moving *vans* driving out of Miss Van Nuys's eyes, and making terribly loud *noises*. So loud that you have to hold your ears. (Get the action in the association.) Van noise –

4 MR SMOLENSKY

5 MR HECHT

9 MISS SMITH

10 MR KANNEN

14 MR SILVERBERG

15 MISS KORNFELD

Van Nuys. Be sure you *see* the picture!

No. 8 is Mr Hamper. Notice the very wide mouth. I would see myself throwing all my dirty clothes into his mouth because it's a hamper. Remember to look at Mr Hamper and *see* the picture in your mind's eye.

No. 9 is Miss Smith. This is a common name, but don't think you'll remember it if you do not make an association. The names Smith, Jones and Cohen are forgotten just as

often as the longer and less common names, and there's less
excuse for doing so. Miss Smith has very full lips, they
almost appear to be swollen. I would see a blacksmith
using a gigantic *smith's* hammer on Miss Smith's lips. The
blows of the hammer are causing the lips to swell. You might
want to utilize Miss Smith's long eyebrows, it doesn't
matter. What *does* matter is that you look at Miss Smith
and *see* that picture or association.

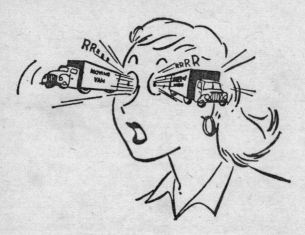

No. 10 is Mr Kannen. Pick an outstanding feature. You
might notice the ear standing out from the head, or the lines
in the corner of the eye, or the thin long mouth. You can
see a *cannon* shooting off the outstanding feature, or
cannons shooting from the feature. Pick the association
you like, and *see* it in your mind's eye.

No. 11 is Mr D'Amico. You can't miss the full head of
wavy hair. See the hair as a *dam*, and it is overflowing while
you scream, 'eek' and 'oh'. Or, you are running towards the
dam shouting, 'me go'. Look at Mr D'Amico, and *see* the
picture.

No. 12 is Miss Forrester. I would see trees (forest)
growing out of those heavy, definite lines on her lower

cheeks. If you want to be sure of the entire name, see the forest growing wild and *tear*ing her cheeks. Forest tear – Forrester. Be sure you *see* the picture.

No. 13 is Mr Pfeffer; the 'p' is silent. The first thing that hits my eye is the cleft in Mr Pfeffer's chin. I would see lots of black *pepper* pouring out of this cleft. So much, in fact, that it's making me sneeze. 'Pepper' would be enough to tell me that this is Mr Pfeffer. If you want to make sure, *hear* yourself sneezing like so: 'fffft', with an 'f' sound. Silly? Yes; but this will come back to you later, and you'll know that the name is Pfeffer, not Pepper. *See* the picture.

No. 14 is Mr Silverberg. See a large silver iceberg instead of Mr Silverberg's jutting chin. Actually see it glittering, so you get the idea of *silver* in there. If you want to use the laugh lines around the corners of Mr Silverberg's mouth, that's O.K., too. See a silver iceberg on each side. Whichever feature you use, be sure actually to *see* the picture.

No. 15 is Miss Kornfeld. I would see millions (exaggeration) of ears of *corn fall*ing from Miss Kornfeld's wide mouth. Make sure that you look at Miss Kornfeld, and actually *see* the picture or association in your mind's eye.

I have purposely used a wide assortment of names to prove that it just doesn't make any difference as to the type of name. You might want to go over these faces once, quickly, to make sure you've made a strong enough association. On pages 128–29 are the same faces in a different order, without their names. See if you can't fill in the fifteen spaces under the pictures. When you've done so, check yourself and be amazed at the improvement in your memory for names and faces!

If you had any trouble at all recalling any of the names, the reason is that you didn't make your association vivid enough; you didn't actually *see* the association in your mind's eye. If you did miss any, just look at the face again, strengthen your association and try it again. You'll surely remember them all on your second try. If you feel confident, why not try that test in Chapter 3, and compare your score

now with the score you originally made. Tomorrow, or the day after, look at the fifteen faces pictured in this chapter and in Chapter 3, and you'll see that you still know the names of all the people!

Keep in mind that if you can remember the names of faces in pictures, you'll find it much easier to do when actually meeting people. Apart from finding an outstanding feature more easily, there are many other things that can

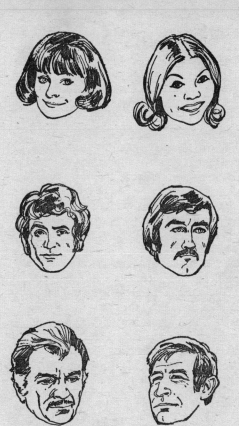

be taken into consideration, such as: manner of speech, speech defects, character, type of walk, manner of bearing, and so on.

If you happened to be at an affair, and wanted to show off by memorizing the names of everyone present, you could do it now, by using the systems you've just learned. You would probably find it helpful to review the names every so often. Each time you look at a person, his name should spring to mind. The name coming to mind in this fashion serves as a review, and serves to etch the name more firmly into your memory. If you were to spot someone you've met, and the name didn't come to mind, ask for the name again, or ask someone else to give it to you. Then strengthen your original association. Try it! You'll amaze yourself and your friends.

For practical purposes – for those of you who meet people, and would like to retain the names – writing the names would help, as far as review is concerned. As I said in the preceding chapters, writing in conjunction with a system of association is fine. This is a good example of that fact. You would, of course, use the systems learned here, upon meeting these people. Then at the end of the day, think of each new person you've met and as the name comes to mind, jot it down. The next day go over this list of names. As you look at each one, a picture of the person's face will come to mind. Just picture the person for a moment, and *see* your original association of the name to face. That's all. Do the same thing a few days later; then again, a week later, and so on until the faces and names are indelibly etched in your memory.

Of course all this is theoretical, because if you wanted to remember these people it is probably because you intend to meet them again. If you do meet them often and recall their names, well, then that serves the purpose of review, and writing the names isn't necessary at all.

The thing to do is to use whatever is best for *you* or your particular circumstances. Just make up your mind to get over the initial effort of actually putting my systems to work, and they will diligently work for you.

18 It pays to remember facts about people

It is the common wonder of all men, how among so many millions of faces there should be none alike. *Sir Thomas Browne*

Yes, fortunately, there are no two faces exactly alike. If all faces did look alike we couldn't remember them or the names, memory system or not. I have been challenged many times to remember the first names of a set of identical twins. So far I have always been able to spot one difference, however minute, in their faces. It is to this difference that I would associate their names. So, as the French say, 'Vive la différence!'

If you have studied the previous chapters on how to remember names and faces, and if you have *tried* the methods, you should be greatly improved by now. Although in most cases it is the second, or family names that most of us want to remember, some of you may be interested in remembering first or Christian names as well. This too can be done with a conscious association. You can use a substitute word for the first name, and get that into your original mental picture; or, you can picture someone you know very well having the same first name with the person you wish to remember.

Substitute words for first names are easy to find: Harry could be 'hairy'; Clark could be 'clock'; for William, I always picture a man with a bow and arrow as William Tell, while money or 'rich' always means Richard, to me. Anne could be 'ant'; Marion could be 'marrying'; for Gloria, you might see the American Flag (Old *Glory*), etc.

If you use the substitute word idea for remembering first names, after a while you will have one at your fingertips for anyone that you meet.

The system of picturing a friend of yours whose first name is the same as the person whom you want to remember might work just as well for you. If you meet a Mr John Sitrous, you could use the substitute word 'citrus' to associate to an outstanding feature; then put your friend, John, into the picture somehow (in a ridiculous way), and you'll remember that Mr Sitrous's first name is John.

Again, it is not for me to tell you which idea to use, you may use one or both, as the circumstances demand. This is entirely up to you. If you find that you can remember first names with one system better than with the other, then by all means use the one that helps you most.

If at first you have a bit of trouble remembering the first names, don't let it bother you; just use the second name. Keep at it for a while and you'll soon be able to remember first names just as well as you do second names, and vice versa. You won't insult anyone by remembering only his or her last name. Benjamin Disraeli had an out even if he forgot both names; he once said, 'When I meet a man whose name I cannot remember I give myself two minutes, then if it is a hopeless case I always say, "And how is the old complaint?" ' Since most of us have some sort of old complaint or other, Disraeli probably flattered everyone he used this on, making them believe that he remembered them quite well. However, no need for subterfuge; use my systems and you will remember names and faces.

More important, I think, than remembering first names is to be able to remember pertinent facts about the people you meet. This holds true for business and social life. Businesswise, particularly, since it is often helpful to remember what items or pattern numbers you sold to a certain customer, or, if you're a doctor, to remember patients' symptoms and ailments, etc. It is also very flattering to meet a person whom you haven't seen in some time and have him ask about things that are close to you, but would ordinarily have no interest to him. This will not only make people like you (people always like you if you show an interest in their interests) but can be quite an asset in business.

The method is the same as for remembering first names. Just put the thing into your original association when you're memorizing the name and face. If I met a Mr Beller, whom I wanted to impress, and I knew he was an avid stamp collector, I might associate 'bell' to an outstanding feature on his face, and then associate stamps to that bell.

Some of you may feel that this might confuse you into thinking that the man's name is Bellstamp; but again, true memory tells you the difference. You'll know that the name is Beller (to make sure, you could use bell-law in the original association) and you'll be able to flatter him by asking, or talking, about his stamp collection.

During my own performances I will usually meet doctors, judges, commissioners, mayors, and many people with titles other than 'Mister'. It is essential for me to address them correctly, because even though I remember their names, people with titles may be insulted if I do not use that title, or if I forget it. The same idea applies; I simply put something into my original association which will remind me of the title. Anything will do; the first object that comes to mind when you hear the title is usually best. I always picture a stethoscope to remind me of 'doctor', because that's the first thing with which I associate a doctor. Of course, scalpel, hypodermic, operating table, or anything like that, would suffice.

When I meet a judge, I always put a gavel into my mental picture. This is enough to remind me to address this person as 'judge'. You might like to picture the judicial robe; that's just as good. Years ago, I recall seeing a picture of New York's mayor Jimmy Walker wearing a top hat. For some reason this picture has always stuck with me. Now, whenever I am introduced to a mayor of a town at an affair, I make sure to get a top hat into my association.

I have done quite a few performances for servicemen, and I have had to prepare a substitute word beforehand to remind me whether the person was a sergeant, corporal, lieutenant, captain, major, or what have you. As I met each man, I would put this substitute word into my association of name to face, and I did address each man correctly.

So you see that any word can be put into your associations to remind you of things pertaining to the person, as well as his or her name. I have mentioned time and again the fact that you must *use* these ideas in order for them to work for you. I do this only because it is important enough to warrant repetition. If you maintain the attitude that nothing can help *your* terrible memory, then nothing will, because you won't let it. Take a positive view of it all; try these ideas, and you'll be pleasantly surprised. If you've read up to here in this book, and tried all the ideas and systems up to now, I'm sure you've already been convinced.

I've also told you that all these ideas and methods are merely aids to your true memory. If you didn't have the capacity to remember to begin with, you wouldn't remember, no matter how many systems you used; nor could you remember the systems. If you were to make an extreme effort to remember, you would; there's no question about that. The problem is that we're all too lazy to make that effort. The systems contained in this book simply make it easier for you to make the effort. In order to make your associations you *must* pay attention to the thing you want to remember; the rest is easy.

It would take far too much time and space for me to tell you how helpful my trained memory has been to me, apart from my public appearances. Of course people will sometimes carry things to an extreme. I meet and remember approximately one to three or four thousand people every week, sometimes more. It would be a little silly for me to try to retain all those names and faces. But I never know when I'll be stopped on the street, or in a cinema, or while driving my car, or in some small town that I may have played two or three years ago – and have someone demand, 'What's my name?'

These people expect me to remember them although I met

them with three or four hundred other people, at the time. The amazing part is that in 20 per cent to 30 per cent of the time, my original associations, made, perhaps years ago, will come back to me after thinking for a few moments. Then I *do* know the person's name. In your case, this is no problem because I'm sure that very few of you have to meet and remember anywhere near three or four hundred thousand people a year.

I think that this book probably would never have been published if it weren't for the fact that I remembered one person's name. I had spoken to Mr Fell, the publisher, about the book the first time I met him. He said he would think about it, and that was that. About five months later, after meeting many thousands of people, I happened to be performing for an all-male group at a charity breakfast. A gentleman approached me and asked if I remembered him. After a moment's thought, I realized it was Mr Fell, who happened to have heard that I was appearing there, and came down to test me. I told him his name; and weeks later he all but confessed that if I hadn't remembered him, he wouldn't have been half as enthused about the book as he was now. You see, he naturally wanted to be sure that my systems really worked.

This is only one instance where remembering one person's name was important to me. Remembering the right person's name at the proper time may perhaps mean a great deal to you sometime in the future. It might be the stepping-stone to a better job, a bigger opportunity or a much better sales contract, etc. So, try these systems, use them, and I believe you'll be well paid for your efforts.

19 It pays to remember telephone numbers

The little girl was trying to get the telephone operator to find a telephone number for her.
OPERATOR: You can find that number in your telephone directory.
LITTLE GIRL: Oh, I can't, I'm standing on it!

Although most of you do not have to stand on the telephone directory in order to use the telephone, you do have to use it quite often to look up numbers that you've forgotten. Sure, many people feel that it isn't necessary to remember telephone numbers since that's *just* what the directory is for; but the fact remains that the post office has to keep information operators on duty continually. Next to forgetting names and faces, I think the most common memory complaint is, 'I simply can't remember telephone numbers!' As I mentioned in an earlier chapter, most untrained memories are one-sided. Those who usually *do* remember telephone numbers can't remember names, and vice versa. Of course, I intend for you to be able to do both, and more, with equal proficiency.

My good friend Richard Himber, famous musician-magician, realized that most people couldn't remember telephone numbers, so he did something about it. He made it very simple for everyone to remember *his* – he just told them to dial his name, R. Himber. Somehow, he managed to obtain an exchange for his telephone that begins with the letters RH. The rest of the number is 4-6237, which you get when you dial i-m-b-e-r. Now, don't you all dial it just to see if this is true – take my word for it, it is!

This, of course, solved everybody's problem when it came to remembering Mr Himber's telephone number (if they remembered his name) but unfortunately we can't all have numbers like this. No, you'll just have to learn to remember telephone numbers, and the telephone operators will love you for it.

Telephone numbers in New York and most major cities consist of an exchange name, an exchange number, and four trunk line numbers, i.e. Columbus 5-6695. By making a ridiculous association of two or three words or items, you can memorize *any* telephone number; and by adding one thought to your association, you can remember *to whom* the telephone number belongs. This system applies to any combination of letters and figures in any telephone number.

Most telephones in use today are dial phones, so all that is necessary to remember is the *first two* letters of the exchange name; since that is all we have to dial. These two letters are all we will consider. Now then, the first thing you have to learn is to form one word which will immediately help you recall both the first two letters of the exchange name *and* the exchange number. The word, of course, should be one that can be pictured easily. The number CO 5-6695 can serve as an example. How can we find one word to represent CO 5? Simple! The word must begin with the letters, 'co', and the very next consonant sound in the word must be the sound that represents the exchange number according to our phonetic alphabet. In this case, it is the 'l' sound, representing 5.

Any word that can be pictured will do, no matter which sounds follow the 'l' sound; because those will be disregarded. The only things that matter in the word you choose are the first two letters and the next consonant sound. For example, the word 'column' would represent CO 5; the 'mn' at the end of the word is disregarded. The words collar, colt, colour, cold or coliseum would also fit the system. If you can think of a word that can be pictured, that has no other letters after the consonant that represents the exchange number – use it. The word 'coal' is an example that fits this case.

Keep in mind that you don't *have* to use a word that has

only the first two letters and the exchange number sound.
The first word that comes to you is usually, although not
always, the one to use. If the number you wish to memorize
begins BEachview 8, you could use the word '*BEef*' (BE 8).
Here are a few more examples to make sure that you get the
idea:

REgent 2 – *rent*   – *Reyn*ard (The Fox)
ESplanade 7 – *esc*ape – *esc*alator
GRamercy 8 – *grav*e – *graph*
DElaware 9 – *deep* – *dep*uty
GOrdon 5 – *gol*d – *goal*
CLover 3 – *cla*m – *clim*b

I've given only two words for each exchange, but there are
many others that would fit.

Do you see how simple it is? There's no reason why you
shouldn't be able to find a word, immediately, to represent
any exchange and exchange number. Let me remind you
that the word you select has to have a meaning for *you* only.
Probably if I gave ten people an exchange and exchange
number they would each use a different word to help
remember it. Although nouns are usually best, that doesn't
mean that you have to use a noun. Some of you may find
that a foreign word you know is just right for a certain
exchange and exchange number; if so, use it; it doesn't
matter. What *does* matter is that it recalls the exchange for
you. I could give you a list of all the exchange names used in
New York City and the exchange numbers used with these
names, and also give you a word that would represent each
of them. I could do that, but I won't. I don't believe it would
help you any. It's much better if you make up the words as
soon as you find it necessary to do so, instead of memorizing
a long list of them.

At the risk of being repetitious I must say, again, that the
picture created in your mind is something that I cannot
help you with. One word may create an entirely different
picture in your mind than it would in mine. Actually,
sometimes it is not even a *word* that I use, but a thought.

I purposely used one in the above examples. For REgent 2 I gave 'Reynard' as a word to help remember it. Now, Reynard creates a definite picture in *my* mind because Reynard the Fox was a favourite character of mine when I was a child. If you never read those wonderful stories, then Reynard would mean nothing to you. If I had used Reynard in my association, I would simply picture a fox. True memory would tell me that the telephone number began RE 2, and *not* FO 7 (fox). I'm telling you all this just to show you that even if you can't think of a word to fit a particular exchange name and number, you can always find something, even a nonsense phrase or word, to recall it for you later on. The same thing holds true not only for telephone numbers, but for *anything* that makes it necessary for you to make up a word for an association.

All right, now to go on with the rest of the telephone number. If you understand the idea of how to make up a word for the exchange name and number, the rest is easy. All you have to worry about now are the four trunk line numbers. Well, any four-digit number can be broken into two of your peg words. If you simply associate the two, you'll remember the four digits. For the number 4298, you would associate rain (42) to puff (98); for 6317 – chum (63) to tack (17); for 1935 – tub to mule, and so on. You now have all the ingredients for remembering telephone numbers, all that remains is to mix them. Let's use CO 5-6695 as an example. To remember this number simply associate coal (CO 5) to choo choo (66) to bell (95)! For the number AL 1-8734 you could use – altar to fog to mower; and for OX 2-4626 – oxen to roach to notch.

Now, before showing you how to remember *whose* telephone number you're remembering, let me point out that there is one fly in the ointment, so to speak, involved here. Were you to make a ridiculous picture in your mind of say steam, rope and tomb, you would know that the exchange was ST 3 (*steam*) and that the trunk line numbers were 4913 (rope, tomb). But would you remember whether it was 4913 *or* 1349? Therein lies the problem! You might be confused a week or so after memorizing a telephone number, as to which peg word was first and which was last. Of course, if you *use* a telephone number that you memorize, then this is really a theoretical problem. Once you've used it a few times you'll *know* which pair of digits comes first. As I've said many times before, the systems are wonderful aids to your true memory. Without the use of the system for remembering telephone numbers you probably wouldn't know *any* of the digits in the number.

However, for numbers that you do *not* intend to use right away there are many methods of avoiding this confusion, some good and some not so good. I'll give you three or four ways right now, and you can pick the one or two that you think best.

The first idea is to make a *link* of the words instead of one complete ridiculous picture. For example, for ST 3-4913 you could make *one* picture of a radiator (steam) lassoing (rope) a tomb; whereas if you made a link you would associate steam to rope, *and then* rope to tomb. Since the link system makes you remember *in sequence*, you would *know* that you've memorized the number in its correct order.

Another idea, and one I use quite often, is to simply make one complete ridiculous picture, but to make the ridiculous picture itself in a logical sequence. Let me explain that for you. Actually I've done it in the example I just gave you. The picture of a radiator lassoing a tomb is quite ridiculous, but it is a good example of a logical sequence in an illogical picture. Having made the association in this way, you couldn't possibly think of tomb being first, or lasso (rope) being second – the words (which, of course, are transposed back to numbers when you want to dial the telephone number) are pictured in the correct order to begin with. Let me give you another example of this so you'll know just what I'm talking about. For the telephone number DE 5-3196 – the words *deal*, *mat* and *beach* would suffice in aiding your memory. If you pictured yourself *deal*ing *mats* on a *beach* (getting sand all over the mats and yourself) you've got a logical illogical association. The

word mat definitely comes before the word beach, so you
know that the number is 3196 and not 9631.

The above idea is the one I use most often, followed by
this one: I always try to find a word to fit *more* than two of
the four digits of the trunk line numbers. For example –
ST 3-4913 – I might picture a radiator ripping the hem of a
girl's dress. Steam–*ripped*–*he*m. Or, steam–*repaid*–*m*e,
etc. And, there will be some numbers wherein you can find a
word to fit all four of the trunk line digits.

I believe that most of you will want to use one or more
of these three methods. However, to give you a wider choice,
here are one or two other ways of avoiding the possibility of
mixing your numbers. You can always use your peg word
for the first two digits of the four; and any word that
is *not* a peg word, but *does* fit phonetically, for the second
pair of digits, i.e. the trunk line number to be memorized is
6491 – use *cherry* for 64, but *don't* use *bat* in your association
for 91 – use any other word for 91, like *beet*, or *boat*. Now,
after any length of time, when you want to remember this
particular number, you would *know* that 64 is first because
cherry is a peg word; beet or boat are *not* peg words,
therefore 91 is the *second* pair of digits! For the number
IN 1-4084, you might associate *ind*ian–rose–fairy. *Fairy* is
not a peg word, so 84 *must* be the last or second two digits.

I devised this last method quite recently and I find that it
works like a charm. Its use definitely dismisses the possibility
of exchanging the numbers. There are other thoughts on the
subject, of course, such as picturing one of your items much
larger than the other, etc., but I don't have too much faith in
them.

I have taken all this space to explain these ideas because
the same thoughts hold true for remembering prices,
addresses, time schedules, pattern numbers and anything
that requires that you memorize four-digit numbers. As far
as telephone numbers are concerned – the worst that could
happen if you exchanged the digits in the trunk line numbers
is that you would dial the wrong number the first time, but
get your party the second time.

By the way, if a zero should be the first of the two digits, simply make up a word for the digits. For 05, use *sail*, *cell* or *sale*; for 07 – *sick*, *sock* or *sack*, etc. If you run across two zeros in a row, you could use *seas*, *sews* or *zoos*.

Well, now you should know how to memorize any telephone number! In order to remember whose telephone number it is, it is necessary to add only *one* word to your association. If the number belongs to someone with whom you deal, say, the tailor, butcher, grocer, doctor, or anyone that can be pictured, just put that person into your association. For example, the tailor's telephone number is FA 4-8862. Just make an association of tailor–*farm*–fife–chain. If you're using my suggestion of not using a peg word for the last two digits, you could use *chin* instead of *chain*. You might picture the tailor (a man sewing) growing fifes on his farm, which he plays with his chin. If you like the *link* idea, simply link the four items.

Since a tailor, doctor, dentist, etc. can be pictured, all you have to do is get that picture into your association. If you want to remember *names* in conjunction with telephone numbers you must use the substitute word system as you learned in Chapter 16. Mr Hayes's telephone number is OR 7-6573 – you might picture a bale of hay (Hayes) playing an *org*an (Or 7) in jail (65) while it combs (73) its hair. If you are using the link idea – link hay to organ, organ to jail, jail to comb. If you like my last suggestion on how to avoid mixing the trunk line numbers change *comb* to coma, game or comma, etc.

Let's say that you wanted to remember that Mr Silverberg's telephone number was JU 6-9950. You might 'see' a picture of a shiny silver iceberg sitting in a courtroom as judge (JU 6) smoking a gigantic *pipe* that's covered with *lace*! This is a logical illogical sequence in one ridiculous picture. I'll use this same number to show how you would handle it using any of the methods for keeping the trunk line numbers straight.

Link method – associate iceberg to judge (the iceberg is pounding his gavel) then judge to pipe ('see' a gigantic pipe *as* a judge) and then pipe to lace (picture yourself smoking a pipe filled with lace, or see a pipe making lace).

If you want to use less items in your association for this particular telephone number you could picture the iceberg as a judge with a lot of *pupils* (9950)!

To use the last method, simply change lace to any other word that would represent 50; like lass, lose, lies or lasso.

I have given you examples of memorizing telephone numbers using the different ideas because I feel that it is up to you to use the method that comes easiest to you. As with anything else in this book I can only give you theoretical examples, your imagination must do the rest for you, and only you can decide which of certain methods are best for you.

I doubt if you would ever find it necessary to memorize a telephone number that you didn't intend to use for any great length of time. The fact that you want to remember it means that you intend to use it. And, as I mentioned before, the association will recall it for you the first few times you have to dial it – after that you can forget your original association, or stop *trying* to remember it, anyway, because the telephone number will probably be permanently etched in your memory.

As usual, the explanation takes much longer than the deed itself. It is but the work of a few moments to memorize a telephone number. Unless you are using it as a memory stunt, and want to do it quickly, you would ordinarily have plenty of time to find the proper words and make your associations. The fact that you *must think* of the number in order to find these words and make the association helps to set it into your mind in the first place. If all I accomplish with this book is to make you think of, or concentrate on, anything you wish to remember – then I will feel that I've accomplished quite a bit, because you will certainly have improved your memory.

You can check your improved memory for telephone numbers right now by trying Test 6 in Chapter 3 again, and comparing the scores.

20 The importance of memory

A businessman travelling in the middle west of America was told about an Indian, living in the vicinity, who had a most fantastic memory. Having just completed a memory course, and priding himself on his own newly acquired achievements, he decided to visit this Indian to see whose memory was better.

He introduced himself to the Indian and proceeded to test him. The memory expert answered every question quickly and accurately. His mind was a storehouse of knowledge, containing such information as the populations of nearly all American cities, important dates, scientific theories, etc. The businessman couldn't stump him. Finally, he decided to try one last question. 'What did you have for breakfast on the morning of April 5th, 1931?'

The Indian didn't hesitate for even a second as he answered, 'Eggs!'

The businessman took his leave, completely stunned by this prodigious memory. When he arrived home he told all his friends about it, only to have them scoff and say that eggs were usually eaten at breakfast, and that anyone could have answered that.

As the years passed, the man began to believe this, until one day he found himself back in the middle west on a sales trip. One afternoon he happened to come upon the same Indian he had met there years ago. Wanting to show that *his* memory for faces was pretty good, he raised his hand in the traditional Indian greeting, and said, 'How.'

The Indian thought for just a moment, and then answered, 'SCRAMBLED!'

Although the above anecdote is pretty silly, since no one would ask anyone to recall what they had for breakfast years ago – you'd be surprised at the questions some people ask me. If I had a conversation with a person some time ago, they'd ask me to repeat the conversation exactly; or, if I'm spied reading a newspaper, someone is sure to grab it from me and insist that I prove that I've memorized it word for word. They don't realize that the beauty of having a trained and systematic memory is that I can remember what I *want* to remember.

It would be kind of ridiculous for me to memorize the daily paper word for word. There is no need for that; however, I can and do remember anything that I come across that I feel is important enough to memorize. I just make an association for it as I read it. When I read a story or novel I am usually reading for enjoyment only, and I'm not at all interested in remembering what I'm reading. There are some things that we all want to forget; for example, it is diplomatic to remember a woman's birthday but not her age.

After completing this book I hope that all of you will be able to remember anything you read, that is, if you want to. As I've mentioned before, you can remember anything if you so desire. These memory systems just make it easier for you. Perhaps some of you do not, as yet, agree with that. You may feel that it is much easier to write down a telephone number than to stop and make an association as I've explained. Well, I must admit that it probably would be faster and easier, at first; but you wouldn't be helping your memory.

You might feel that since there are millions of reference books to use whenever you need certain information, why bother to remember. And, of course, most businessmen have secretaries to remember for them.

Yes, it's true that businessmen have secretaries, but they probably wouldn't be in the position to hire one if they didn't have good memories for their businesses in the first place. *And*, how long do you think the secretary would keep the job if *she* couldn't remember?

Although there are millions of reference books, and we certainly need them – a lawyer pleading a case in court would much rather have the details of a precedent in his

memory than have to stop to look it up. If he could quote
pages and laws from certain law books, the judge and jury
would most certainly be favourably impressed. A carpenter
doesn't stop to look at a book when he has to use a
particular tool; he remembers how to use it. If an emergency
arises on the operating table, the surgeon acts immediately.
All the medical books in existence wouldn't help that
patient if the doctor didn't remember just what to do. When
you visit your doctor and tell him the symptoms of your
illness, he doesn't have to refer to the notes he wrote while
attending medical school – he remembers which ailment has
which symptoms.

Those that write new ideas on old subjects must know or
remember all the old ideas first. Could a man like Professor
Einstein come up with new formulas and theories if he
didn't know or remember all the current ones? Of course
not. The telephone would never have been invented if
Alexander Graham Bell had not known or remembered all
the principles of transporting sound that were then in
existence. If it were not for memory we would never have
new inventions.

I could go on, *ad infinitum*, demonstrating how and why
the memory is important; or why it is not always
convenient to refer to books or lists. Almost everything we
do is based on memory. The things we often say we do by
'instinct' are really done through memory.

Writing things down just isn't enough in itself to help you
remember. Why are some children slow in school, even
though they write notes in class? It is *not* because they are
stupid! It is because they don't remember their work. In
school they are told they must remember certain things, but
unfortunately, they are not taught *how* to do so.

So, a trained and retentive memory is certainly
important.

It is getting over the first hurdle that is always the most
difficult in any new thing you learn. The first hurdle in
training your memory is to actually use my system. Use it
and it'll work for you. Just knowing the system and still

writing telephone numbers on paper is the same as not knowing the system at all.

Those of you who happen to know how to type fairly rapidly – do you recall how you felt when you first started to learn typing? You thought you'd never get the hang of it, and felt that others, who did type well, were just more suited for it than you were. Now, you probably can't understand why you felt that way; there is nothing more natural than for you to sit down and type rapidly. Well, it's the same with a trained memory. I believe that I can memorize a telephone number faster than anyone can write it, and, I strengthen my memory each time I do so. When I first started using these systems, I felt as you may feel now; that it is easier to write things down and forget them than to bother with associations. But, keep at it, and you'll feel the same about this as you do about typing. You'll wonder, after a while, why it took any effort at all in the beginning.

The thing to keep in mind, above all else, is to make all your associations ridiculous and/or illogical. Many of the systems being taught today, and those in the past, do not stress this nearly enough. As a matter of fact, some of them will teach you to make logical associations. There's only one fault with such systems as far as I'm concerned – they won't work. I do not believe that you can remember logical associations anywhere as well, or as easily, as ridiculous ones.

Some of the old systems taught the student to *correlate* two objects when he wanted to remember one in conjunction with the other. A correlation meant to link the two objects by means of other words which either sounded alike, meant the same, were the exact opposites or were brought to mind somehow or other. This happens to be an excellent imagination exercise, so let me explain it to you. If you wanted to remember 'pencil' and light 'bulb' for some reason, you might reason this way:

pencil–lead–heavy–light–*bulb*.

Do you see the process? Pencil would naturally make you

think of lead; the mineral lead is very heavy; the opposite of heavy is light; and light logically leads you to bulb.

How would you correlate 'diamond' to 'cigarette'? Well, here's one way: diamond–ring–smoke ring–smoke–cigarette. Actually, you can correlate any two objects to each other; even the most unlikely things. Of course, it's much easier to remember 'pencil' and 'bulb' by making an association of yourself writing with a light bulb instead of a pencil; or, throwing a switch, and a pencil lights instead of a bulb. As far as 'diamond' and 'cigarette' is concerned, if you 'saw' yourself smoking a diamond instead of a cigarette you'd certainly recall it with more facility than by making a correlation. I mention the correlations only because it *is* a good imagination exercise, and because you might have some fun trying it with your friends. The idea, of course, is to use as few words as possible in order to correlate any two items.

Correlations are a fairly current idea for memory training, but as I've already told you, memory systems go back as far as early Greek civilization. I believe it was Simonides, the Greek poet, who first used something like the Peg system in the year 500 B.C. He used the different rooms of his house, and the pieces of furniture in the various rooms, as his pegs. This is limited, but it *will* work. If you would make up your mind to use the rooms of your house and the furniture in a definite order, you would have a list of peg words. These would be the things you already know or remember, and any new thing to be memorized would be associated to them.

This must have worked for Simonides, because one of the stories about him tells of the time he was giving a recitation at a banquet, and the roof of the building collapsed. Everyone was killed, except Simonides. Because of the mangled condition of the bodies they could not be identified for burial. Simonides was able to tell just who each one was; for he had memorized their *positions* around the banquet table.

Coming back to modern times – General George Marshall

received some favourable publicity because of something he did at some of his press conferences. He told the newsmen to interrupt him and ask him any questions, at any time during his talk. The reporters would do that, asking questions pertaining to the topic that the General was discussing at that moment. General Marshall would listen to the question, but would not answer it. He wouldn't break his train of thought, but went right on with his talk. After the talk was completed, he would look at one of the men who had asked a question, and answer that particular one. He would then look at another man, and answer his question. He did this until all or most of the questions were answered. This was always of great amazement to the newsmen; but it is quite easy with the aid of a memory system.

Former U.S. Postmaster James Farley has a reputation of knowing some twenty thousand people by their first names. In a recent article for the *New York Times* Mr Farley called remembering names the 'most effective of all forms of flattery'. His marvellous memory for names has certainly been a great help to him. It is even said that Mr Farley's campaigning and calling people by name was influential towards the late Franklin Roosevelt's first election to the presidency.

I don't expect you all to be influential in the election of presidents, but you can certainly improve your memory beyond your wildest hopes, if you will learn and *use* the systems taught in this book.

21 Don't be absent-minded

Towards the conclusion of his lecture on the wonderful sights to
be seen in this world the famous traveller said, 'There are some
spectacles that one never forgets!'
At this point a tiny old lady in the back row stood up and
timidly inquired, 'Oh, my, can you tell me where I could get a
pair? I'm always forgetting mine!'

Are *you* continually plagued by misplacing certain items?
Do you waste precious time searching for *your* glasses or for
the pencil which is usually perched behind your ear? Are
you the type that's always screaming, 'But I just had it in my
hands a moment ago!'? Do you always hide your valuable
trinkets so well that you yourself can't find them? Ladies,
are you constantly late for a date because you simply can't
locate your favourite lipstick? And, men, does your wife
rant and scream while you laboriously search for that
misplaced cuff link?

If the answer to any of these questions is 'Yes', run, don't
walk, to your nearest bookstore . . .

Well, if this *were* a radio or television commercial, it
might sound something like that, don't you think? But
seriously, have I hit the bull's eye with some of the above
questions? I'm almost certain that I have, because very few
of us are fortunate enough not to be absent-minded at
times.

Many people make the mistake of confusing
absent-mindedness with a poor memory. Actually, I feel
that they should be considered as two entirely different
things. People with excellent memories can also be
absent-minded. You've all heard of the absent-minded
professor stories; well, be assured that in order to be a

professor you must have a good memory to begin with. The hundreds of gags about the absent-minded professors who wind their wives, kiss the cat goodnight and put out the clock may be true for all I know, but it still doesn't signify that they have poor memories.

I believe that you can cure absent-mindedness with just a little effort and with the tips contained in this chapter. However, please do not feel that you can do it by just *reading* it. You have to make it your business to *use* the information supplied here. Then, and only then, will it help you. I assume that many people will read through a book of this type, never try to use the information given, and then complain that this will never help them. That, of course, will be true if you just read through this book without attempting to apply the systems. Many adults always claim that they are too old to learn. I believe they mean that they are too *lazy* to learn – no one is too old! E. L. Thorndike, an authority on adult education, said that 'age is no handicap to learning a new trade, profession, or anything you *want* to do at any time of life'. The italics in this quote are mine; if you really *want* to learn, you can; so don't use age as an excuse.

Actually, absent-mindedness is nothing more than inattention. If you paid attention to where you put your glasses, naturally you would know where they were when you needed them. The American College Dictionary gives 'preoccupied' as one of the definitions of absent-minded, and that just about hits the nail on the head. The little things that we do continually, like putting down things, are just not important enough to occupy our minds – so, we become absent-minded.

It stands to reason that if you put things away without thinking, or mechanically, you'll forget where they are, because you never remembered in the first place. When you leave your house, you usually worry about whether you locked your door or not, simply because you locked it unconsciously without giving it a thought.

So, I've solved your problem! To avoid absent-mindedness, *think* what you're doing. I know, you're thinking, 'I knew that. If I were able to think each time I put something away, or locked a door, I wouldn't be absent-minded!' Well, then, why not use conscious associations to help you remember trivial things? You can, you know, and it's easy to do.

For example, one thing that is annoying to all of us is forgetting to post letters. You either forget to take them when you leave your house, or, if you do take them, they remain in your pocket for days. If you want to be sure that you take the letter with you when you leave the house, do this: first decide what it is that you do or see at the very last moment upon leaving your house. I personally see the doorknob of my front door, because I check it to see if the door is locked. That is the last thing I do, so I make a ridiculous association between doorknob and letter. When I leave my house the next morning, I'll check the doorknob; once I think of doorknob, I'll recall my ridiculous association and remember that I must take the letter!

The last thing that you do before you leave your house may be entirely different; you may kiss your wife or husband goodbye – well, associate that kiss with the letter. Make sure that your associations are ridiculous and/or illogical.

Now, how can you be sure to *post* the letter? One way is

to keep it in your hand until you drop it in a pillar box. If you'd rather keep it in your pocket, make an association between the person the letter is going to, and the pillar box. You might 'see' him sitting on top of a pillar box, etc. If you do not know the person well enough to picture, use a substitute word as you've already learned. If the letter were going to the telephone company, you would associate telephone to pillar box, and so on. When you see a pillar box, in the street, it will remind you to post the letter. (After all that, I hope you remembered to put a stamp on the envelope!)

This idea can be used for all the little things you want to remember to do. If you keep forgetting your umbrella at the office, just associate umbrella to the last thing you do upon leaving the office. If your wife calls and tells you to be sure to buy some eggs on your way home – associate eggs with, say, your front door. This will act as a final reminder. Instead of waiting to be reminded when you're home, associate eggs to grocery store; then when you see a grocery store, it will remind you to go in and buy the eggs.

Of course, all these are theoretical examples: you would know just what to associate to what, in your own particular case.

Now we come to the real petty annoyances of absent-mindedness; such as putting things down, and then forgetting where they are. Well, the method applied to this is exactly the same. You have to make an association between the object and its location. For instance, if the phone rings, and as you reach for it you put your pencil behind your ear – make a fast mental picture between ear and pencil. When you're through with the phone, and you think of pencil, you will know it's behind your ear. The same thing goes for any small item or small errand. If you're in the habit of putting things down anywhere, get into the habit of making an association to remind you of where it is.

One of the questions usually asked at this point is: 'Fine, but how am I going to remember to make these associations for all these petty things?' There is only one answer to this question – use some will-power at first, and be sure that you *do* make the associations. When you see the results, I'm sure you'll manage to keep it up and, before you know it, you will have acquired the habit.

There is no doubt, by the way, that this system *must* cure absent-mindedness. The reason is obvious; the eyes cannot see if the mind is absent – and your mind is absent when you put things away mechanically. The very idea of making an association *makes* you think of what you're doing for at least a fraction of a second, and that's all that's necessary. If you make an association between your key and your door, as you lock the door – you are no longer doing it mechanically. You are thinking of it; therefore, later on when you wonder if you locked the door, you'll *know* you did. When setting the alarm on your clock, make an association between clock and hand, or between clock and anything, for that matter. It doesn't matter; the important thing is that you're thinking of it for the moment. And, because you did think of it for the moment, you won't have to get out of bed later to check if the alarm is set.

I say that the association doesn't matter, and it doesn't. As a matter of fact, if you closed your eyes and saw yourself turning off your iron as you were doing it, you wouldn't have to worry about whether it was on or off, while trying to enjoy a film. Closing the eyes and picturing the action is just as good as the association. It serves the same purpose: that of forcing you to think of what you're doing at the moment.

That's all there is to it. But I can't stress strongly enough the necessity of using what you've just learned. Please don't read it, nod your head and say it's a great idea, and then forget about it. Put out the bit of effort necessary at first, and you will be glad you did.

Captain of ship, talking to sailor: 'Don't you ever say "the back of the ship" again – that's the *stern* of the ship; and that's port-side, that's starboard, that's the crow's nest, that's the gig, that's the forecastle, etc.

'If you ever say "back of the ship" again, I'll throw you out of that – that, er, that little round hole over there!'

Just as absent-mindedness is often mistaken for a poor memory, so is absent-mindedness often blamed for mental blocks. Again, I don't think that one has anything to do with the other. Having something familiar on the tip of your tongue and not being able to remember it is not absent-mindedness. What it is and why it happens, I don't know; but unfortunately it does happen; to me as well as to you.

There isn't much I can do to help avoid mental blocks. There isn't any system I know of that can stop them. However, I can tell you that when it does happen – try to think of events associated with the name or event you're trying to recall. If it's the name of a familiar person that you can't think of, try to picture the last time you saw that person, where it was, what you were doing and who else was present at the time.

The mind must work in its own devious way; more often than not just thinking *around* the fact you want will make it pop into your mind.

If this doesn't help, the next best thing is to forget about it. Stop thinking about it completely for a while, and the odds are it will come to you when you least expect it.

That's about all the help I can give you when it comes to mental blocks. Try my suggestions the next time it happens to you; you may be surprised at how helpful they are!

22 Amaze your friends

FARMER (showing off his farm to a friend): 'How many sheep would you say were in that flock? See if you can get close with a rough guess.'
FRIEND (after short pause): 'I'd say there were about 497 sheep there.'
FARMER 'Why, you hit it right on the head, that's exactly right! How in the world did you know?'
FRIEND 'It was simple, really, I just counted all the legs, and then divided by four!'

The memory stunt contained in this chapter may not be as astounding as dividing the legs of sheep by four, but it's certainly easier to do. You'll probably be glad to know that there are no mathematics involved at all – just a trained memory.

A friend of mine in the textile business in New York has told me that he has gained quite a reputation for himself by remembering numbers. He goes to lunch with a few business acquaintances each day, and he invariably asks them to give him any four- or five-digit number to memorize. He usually has anywhere from three to six people with him, and he memorizes the numbers they give him. They interrupt him during the luncheon to see if he can still recall the numbers and, of course, he does.

I don't mention this because it's particularly wonderful, but it is a good conversation starter, and it has accomplished a purpose for my friend. He tells me that everyone in his trade is talking about him and his remarkable memory. I *do* mention it, however, to show you how people are impressed with any sort of memory feat; only because they feel that they could never accomplish it themselves. If people are so amazed when a man remembers a half-dozen four- or five-digit numbers, you can imagine the fantastic effect upon them, after you've mastered the stunt contained in these pages.

How would you like to be able to memorize this list of numbers:

	1	2	3	4	5	6	7	8	9	10
A –	9491	0261	4850	8210	1427	0214	5390	0141	7450	7590
B –	2195	6140	5827	5197	4270	9401	4260	5014	1395	8150
C –	8520	7461	9511	7157	9420	4532	1950	1404	7841	7410
D –	2116	5152	9470	2154	9750	7471	7220	1941	0191	3102
E –	4595	5891	3944	0182	0594	9414	6720	8227	8527	7480
F –	0137	5814	9950	9427	1285	2754	3662	1540	8927	9521
G –	9015	3145	8195	8540	9514	7040	7312	1211	9227	1270
H –	9210	7427	0216	4910	7531	7421	1484	2469	0791	2520
I –	4175	1842	3058	7462	3212	0746	7915	7527	0743	9710
J –	4112	9434	0941	7212	9402	7213	5810	1204	6920	4210

That's right! You *can* memorize this list of four hundred digits, easily! Not only will you know them in order, but also out of sequence! The idea is to give anyone a copy of this list, and have them test you on it. They may ask you to give the numbers across for letter G, or the numbers down for column 4. They can ask for E7, and you will immediately give them the number 6720. In other words, you prove to them that you have thoroughly memorized the list; and so you have!

My good friend and memory expert, Bernard Zufall, was the first one that I know of to use this type of stunt. He has been using it for many years with three-digit numbers instead of the four-digit numbers that appear here. He, of course, utilized his own methods to memorize the list. I will teach you here the method that I use:

You must realize by now that it would be almost impossible to accomplish this without the aid of the phonetic alphabet. Certainly, it would be definitely impossible to memorize and *retain* the numbers without it. As a matter of fact, this feat is so unbelievable to the uninitiated, that you will find some people examining the list to find some mathematical solution. Let them; since this is not based on mathematics at all, they'll be more impressed and confused than ever.

None of the four-digit numbers in the list is repeated at any time, each one is used only once. The numbers have not been chosen at random. I've picked each one because it fits into the system. And here is the system: if someone were to call E7 – here is the way my mind would work. My Key word for E7 must begin with the letter E, and it must have one other *consonant* sound at the end. That sound (in this particular case) must be the sound that represents 7, which is the k or hard g sound. My Key word for E7 is 'egg'. Eggs come from chickens – and the phonetic alphabet tells me that 'chickens' stands for 6720. If you'll check the list, you will see that 6720 is the correct number!

If B5 were called, I would know that the Key word must begin with the letter B, and the ending consonant sound must be the l sound for 5. The Key word for B5 is 'bell'. A bell rings. *Rings* – 4270! Can you see the simplicity of it? Don't get me wrong – it will take you a bit of time and study to master all the numbers, but the system *is* easy. Again, may I mention that this is not only a fantastic memory stunt, but a wonderful thinking and memory exercise. Each time you master one of the stunts in this book, whether you care to present them or not, you are improving your memory, exercising that muscle and sharpening your wits.

Well then, you know that each time a letter and number are called, you must transpose it into a Key word. It doesn't matter if the number is called first, the system is the same. The letter is always at the beginning and the consonant sound that represents the number is at the end of the word. This Key word is correlated to, or associated with, another word; and this word gives you the four-digit number, according to the phonetic alphabet. If someone were to call '8C', you would know that the Key word starts with C and ends with the f or v sound. The Key word is 'cuff'. Cuff is correlated to trouser. *Trouser* – 1404!

The entire list for the one hundred four-digit numbers follows here. After you have looked them over, I'll explain some more about the presentation of the feat.

A1 – ate-burped	F1 – fat-stomach
A2 – awn-sunshade	F2 – fun-laughter
A3 – aim-rifles	F3 – foam-bubbles
A4 – air-vents	F4 – fur-bearing
A5 – ale-drink	F5 – foil-tinfoil
A6 – ash-cinder	F6 – fish-angler
A7 – ache-limps	F7 – fake-magician
A8 – Ave-street	F8 – five-dollars
A9 – ape-growls	F9 – fib-fibbing
A10 – ace-clubs	F10 – fuse-blend
B1 – bat-and ball	G1 – gat-pistol
B2 – bean-shooters	G2 – gown-material
B3 – bum-loafing	G3 – game-football
B4 – boar-wild pig	G4 – grow-flowers
B5 – bell-rings	G5 – gall-bladder
B6 – badge-breast	G6 – gush-geysers
B7 – bag-oranges	G7 – gag-comedian
B8 – buff-lustre	G8 – gave-donated
B9 – baby-dimple	G9 – gap-opening
B10 – bass-fiddles	G10 – gas-tanks
C1 – cat-felines	H1 – hat-bands
C2 – can-crushed	H2 – hen-crowing
C3 – comb-bald head	H3 – ham-sandwich
C4 – car-Cadillac	H4 – hare-rabbits
C5 – coal-burns	H5 – hill-climbed
C6 – cash-real money	H6 – hash-corned
C7 – coke-tables	H7 – hack-driver
C8 – cuff-trouser	H8 – have-ownership
C9 – cap-covered	H9 – hop-skipped
C10 – case-crates	H10 – hose-nylons
D1 – dot-and dash	I1 – it-article
D2 – den-wild lion	I2 – inn-tavern
D3 – dam-breaks	I3 – I'm-myself
D4 – deer-antler	I4 – Ira-Gershwin
D5 – dill-pickles	I5 – isle-Manhattan
D6 – dish-cracked	I6 – itch-scratch
D7 – dog-canines	I7 – Ike-Capitol
D8 – dove-white bird	I8 – ivy-cling
D9 – dope-stupid	I9 – (y)ipe-scream
D10 – dose-medicine	I10 – ice-buckets

E1 – eddy-whirlpool	J1 – jot-write down
E2 – en-alphabet	J2 – John-Barrymore
E3 – em-emperor	J3 – jam-spread
E4 – err-is divine	J4 – jar-contain
E5 – eel-slippery	J5 – jail-prison
E6 – edge-border	J6 – judge-condemn
E7 – egg-chickens	J7 – jack-lifts
E8 – eve-evening	J8 – jive-dancer
E9 – ebb-falling	J9 – Jap-Japanese
E10 – ess-curves	J10 – juice-rinds

You'll notice that there is only one slight exception in the
system, at I9. There is no word beginning with I and ending
with the p or b sound. So I use the word 'yipe', which serves
the purpose just as well. Also, in every possible case, the
sounds representing the four-digit numbers are contained in
one word. There are only eight instances where I found it
necessary to use a phrase of two words.

I'm sure that you all can see the simple associations or
correlations with each Key word. If you go over them once
or twice, concentrating on them as you do, you should
remember most of them. Each Key word should lead you
logically to the associated word. Coke, for C7, is short for
Coca-Cola, which is usually found on dinner *tables*. En, for
E2, is just the name of the letter itself, which is part of
the *alphabet*. I don't think that any of the others need any
explaining.

You must learn all these words thoroughly before you can
present this feat for your friends. After you've learned them,
practise the transposing of the associated words or phrases
into numbers. Once you can do that quickly, you're ready
to present the feat.

You can have the list printed on a card, if you like, so that
you can hand them out to your friends. Then after you've
demonstrated your fabulous powers of retention and recall,
you can let them keep the card as a souvenir. Let them try
to memorize it, if they can!

Apart from simply allowing your spectators to call the
letter and number, you can go further. They can ask you to

call out all the numbers diagonally from, say, A1 to J10. All you have to do is give the numbers for A1, B2, C3, D4, etc. They might ask for row F backwards – you just give them F10, F9, F8, etc. If they want the four-digit numbers backwards also, you can do that too. For example, you know the associated word for F10 (fuse) is *blend* – instead of giving the number 9521, give it as 1259! F9 is fibbing – backwards the number is 7298, and so on.

If you're asked to give row 6 backwards, simply call off, J6, I6, H6, G6 down, or up, to A6. I know that it is difficult for some people to work backwards with the alphabet. I can solve that problem for you, easily. You can learn the representative number of any letter in the alphabet by utilizing the first twenty-six peg words in conjunction with a representative adjective. This is what I mean:

Awful tie	Neat tyre
Brave Noah	Old towel
Cute ma	Pleasing dish
Damp rye	Quiet tack
Excellent law	Red dove
Funny shoe	Solid tub
Guernsey cow	Tough nose
Heavy ivy	Ugly net
Idle bee	Virtuous nun
Jagged toes	Wonderful name
Korean tot	X-rayed Nero
Loud tin	Yellow nail
Marble tomb	Zig-zag notch

Notice that the adjective for the peg word for 3 begins with the third letter of the alphabet 'c'; the 10th adjective begins with the tenth letter 'j', etc. If you make a quick picture in your mind of each of these, you will know the position, numerically, of all the letters! Of course you can use any adjective you like, as long as it begins with the proper letter. If you wanted to know the position, say, of the letter 'o' – just think of the adjective that you used: *old towel*. You know that 'towel' is 15, therefore 'o' is the fifteenth letter of the alphabet.

You can use this idea, or, elsewhere in this book (Chapter 12) you will find an idea of how to use the twenty-six letters themselves in order to have a list of twenty-six secondary peg words. You can tie these words to your basic peg words, and you will have accomplished the same thing. You will know the numerical positions of all the letters.

Either one of these methods will enable you to use the letters of the alphabet to a much better advantage. Just thinking backwards from peg word 26 to peg word 1 will make it easy for you to recite the entire alphabet backwards. This in itself is a good stunt, since most people cannot recite the alphabet backwards, without quite a bit of effort. However, the important thing is that this idea will be of use when you're asked to give a numbered row backwards; or diagonally from J10 to A1, or J1 to A10.

After doing this stunt for a while, you will find that eventually you will not even think of your Key words and associations! As soon as a letter and number is called, the four-digit number will pop into your mind.

That is the beauty of mnemonics, it is just an aid to your true memory. It is a means to an end, and once you've reached or acquired that end, you can forget the means!

23 It pays to remember appointments and schedules

'The man who is always punctual in keeping appointments never loses anything by it.'
'No, only about half an hour waiting for the other fellow to show up.'

There isn't much I can do about those of you who know that you have an appointment, and get there late, anyway. But I think I can help you if you forget those appointments completely. You've already learned, in a previous chapter, how to remember your errands or appointments for each day. You can still use that idea; but if, in your particular business, or even socially, you find it necessary to keep numerous appointments during the week at certain times of day, you'll be interested in this chapter. The system contained here is one which enables you to make a conscious association as soon as you've made an appointment. By making this association, you can recall all your appointments for each day of the week without bothering with a date or memo book.

For those of you who don't care about remembering weekly appointments or schedules, I would suggest that you learn the idea behind the method anyway. You never know when you might find it useful. Please don't let the length of the explanation frighten you; once you understand and use it, there's nothing to it.

The first thing you must do is to give a number to each day of the week. Since there are seven days in the week, you'll number them from 1 to 7. According to our calendar, Sunday is the first day of the week; but I have found that many people refer to Monday as the first day. This, I imagine, is because of our work-a-day world, and the first

day of work is Monday. I will therefore use Monday as the
first day in the following explanation. If you are accustomed
to considering Sunday as the first day of the week, just
change the explanation as you read. From now on
remember the days of the week in this manner:

Monday   – 1
Tuesday   – 2
Wednesday – 3
Thursday   – 4
Friday   – 5
Saturday   – 6
Sunday   – 7

Once you know the number of each day of the week you
can transpose any day at any hour to *one* of your peg words.
That's right, you will use the peg words which you already
know, to help you remember schedules and appointments.
Each day at every hour will be represented by a peg word,
and you don't have to remember anything to know the
words; it works itself.

Any day at any particular hour can be transposed into a
two-digit number in this way: the number of the day will
be the first digit, and the hour itself will be the second digit.
For example, if you wanted to remember an appointment for
Wednesday at 4.00 o'clock – Wednesday is the third day, so
3 is the first digit. The appointment is for 4.00 o'clock, so
4 is the second digit. You now have a two-digit number – 34,
and the peg word for 34 is 'mower'. Therefore, 'mower' must
represent Wednesday at 4.00 o'clock!

Monday at 2.00 o'clock would be 'tin'. Monday is the
first day, and the time is 2.00 o'clock. In the same way, you
would arrive at the following:

Thursday at 1.00 o'clock – rod (41)
Friday at 8.00 o'clock   – lava (58)
Sunday at 6.00 o'clock   – cage (76)
Tuesday at 9.00 o'clock – knob (29)

Simple, isn't it? Of course if you can transpose the day
and hour to a peg word, it is just as easy to transpose a peg

word to the day and hour. 'Notch', for example, is your peg word for 26; so it must represent Tuesday (2) at 6.00 o'clock.

There are two hours that cannot be represented by a peg word. That is because they themselves are composed of two digits. I mean, of course, 11.00 and 12.00 o'clock. Ten o'clock *can* be transposed to a regular peg word, because it is thought of as zero only, instead of one and zero. In other words, Saturday at 10.00 o'clock would be transposed to 60 (cheese), because Saturday is the sixth day and 10.00 o'clock is zero. 'Rose' (40) would represent Thursday at 10.00 o'clock; Monday at 10.00 o'clock is 'toes', and so on.

I'll give you two methods for handling eleven and twelve o'clock, both of which have been tried and tested. The first method is the obvious one (although not the better one) because it follows the same system as the other hours. Transpose any day at eleven or twelve o'clock to a *three*-digit number by adding the 11 or 12 on to the number of the day e.g. Tuesday at 11.00 o'clock – 211; Thursday at 12.00 o'clock – 412; Sunday at 12.00 o'clock – 712; Wednesday at 11.00 o'clock – 311, etc. Now, you would have to make up a peg word, following the phonetic alphabet, which would fit each day at eleven or twelve o'clock. The words you select would be used all the time for those days and hours. If you want to use this idea (don't make up your mind until you've read the second method) I'll give you some examples of words that can be used. You can pick any of these, or any that you find by yourself.

Monday	11.00 – dotted, toted	
	12.00 – tauten, tootin'	
Tuesday	11.00 – knotted, knitted	
	12.00 – Indian, noddin'	
Wednesday	11.00 – mated, imitate	
	12.00 – mutton, mitten	
Thursday	11.00 – raided, radiate	
	12.00 – rotten, written	
Friday	11.00 – lighted, loaded	
	12.00 – Latin, laden	

Saturday	11.00 – cheated, jaded
	12.00 – jitney, shut in
Sunday	11.00 – coated, cadet
	12.00 – kitten, cotton

The following method, I think, is the better. First of all
I transpose the day at 11.00 or 12.00 o'clock into a two-digit
instead of a three-digit number. I do this by considering
11.00 o'clock as a one, and 12.00 o'clock as a two. Now,
Friday at 11.00 o'clock is thought of as 51; Friday at
12.00 o'clock – 52; Sunday at 11.00 o'clock – 71; Sunday at
12.00 o'clock – 72, etc. Of course, you can't use your regular
peg words for these, since they are already being used for one
and two o'clock; so use any other word, that fits
phonetically, for these numbers.

Let me give you a few examples. For Tuesday at 11.00
o'clock you could use the word 'nut'; later on, when you
picture your association (I'll explain the associations in a
moment) you will know that 'nut' couldn't represent
Tuesday at 1.00 o'clock because you would have used your
regular peg word 'net' for that. So 'nut' must stand for
Tuesday at 11.00 o'clock.

Saturday at 12.00 o'clock could be represented by 'chin'.
Your regular peg word 'chain' represents Saturday at 2.00
o'clock, so you know that 'chin' must mean Saturday at
12.00. Do you get it, now? Basically, it's this: for any day
at eleven or twelve o'clock use the same *sounds* that you
would use for that day at one or two o'clock, but do *not* use
your regular peg word. That's all there is to that!

If all your appointments are usually made for the exact
hour, on the hour, you actually need read no further about
memorizing appointments; you have all the information you
need right now. Supposing you have an appointment to see
your dentist at 9.00 o'clock on Tuesday, and you want to be
sure that you won't forget it. Well, transpose Tuesday at
9.00 o'clock to the peg word 'knob', and associate that to
dentist. You might picture a gigantic doorknob as a dentist,
or you could see (and feel) your dentist pulling a knob from
your mouth, instead of a tooth.

If you had to remember to make a deposit at your bank on Monday at 2.00 o'clock – you would associate 'tin' to bank. You have to catch a plane on Friday at 11.00 o'clock – associate 'loaded' or 'lad' (according to the method you're using for 11.00 and 12.00 o'clock) to aeroplane. Wednesday at 10.00 o'clock you have to visit a friend – associate 'mice' to your friend, etc.

If you usually have appointments with people whom you do not know too well, or if you cannot picture them, use a substitute word for their names in your associations.

That's all you have to do. If you have made an association for all your appointments for an entire week, and you want to remember what you have scheduled for, say, Tuesday – simply go over the peg words for that particular day: Tuesday – nose, net, nun, name, Nero, nail, notch, neck, knife, knob, knitted or knot, and Indian or neon. As soon as you reach a peg word that has been associated, you'll know it! You might reach 'neck', and know immediately that you've made a picture of neck, and say hospital. This will remind you that you have to visit a sick friend at the hospital at 7.00 o'clock on Tuesday! That's all! Again, you need only try it to be convinced that it works.

As far as I personally am concerned, this is all I use to remember my weekly schedule. Some of my appointments may be arranged for the hour exactly, and others for, say, 3.15, 3.30 or 3.45, but I find that it doesn't matter. If I associate the day of the appointment at 3.00 o'clock, on the hour, true memory tells me that the date is for fifteen, thirty or forty-five minutes past the hour. However, there may be some of you who must remember the exact time, to the minute, for some appointments, such as catching trains, etc. In order to do this, you must add only one word to your mental picture. You would actually be remembering a four-digit instead of a two-digit number.

The second pair of digits will represent minutes, while the first two digits represent the day and the hour. For example, if your appointment with the dentist was on Tuesday at 9.42 o'clock – transpose the day and hour to 'knob' (29), and get 'rain' into the association to represent 42. You realize, of course, that in this case you are faced with the same problem as you were when learning to memorize the four trunk line digits of a telephone number.

In the above example, how will you be sure that your dental appointment is for Tuesday at 9.42, and not for Thursday at 2.29 ? This could happen if you weren't sure as to which peg word belongs first, and which belongs last. Well, the problem is solved in the same manner as it was solved for telephone numbers. The best solution is to make a 'logical illogical' association, so that, even though it is a ridiculous picture, one peg *must* logically follow another.

If you made a picture of your dentist pulling a 'knob' from your mouth, instead of a tooth, and doing it in the pouring 'rain', you would know that knob came first, followed by rain. Any of the other suggestions that I gave you for telephone numbers will apply for appointments, too. If you used the Link for your picture – you would associate dentist to knob and then knob to rain. The idea of using a word other than the regular peg word for the last two digits (in this case, the digits representing the minutes) is just as applicable here. That would help for any day at any time, except 11.00 or 12.00 o'clock, where it wouldn't be necessary, since you are not using a regular peg for the day and time, anyway.

You are the best judge as to just which ideas to use. I would suggest trying them all; the one that comes easiest to you, of course, is the right one for you. Although, as I told you, I don't think it necessary to bother with the minutes of an appointment – if I did want to remember the minutes, I would do it this way. On Monday at 3.25 I must remember to pick up a television set – I would picture a television set acting as a 'tomb' stone, while 'nails' perform on the screen.

You see, I use the logical illogical picture idea. The association above will leave no doubt that 'tomb' (Monday at 3.00 o'clock) comes first, followed by 'nail' (25 minutes). One other example: on Wednesday at 12.10 I have a date to go swimming – I would make a picture of myself swimming; I hit a 'mine' which injures my 'toes'. Now, when I go over my pegs for Wednesday of that week: mice, mat, moon, mummy, mower, mule, match, mug, movie, map, mitt and mine (I always use 'mitt' to represent Wednesday at 11.00, and 'mine' for Wednesday at 12.00), I will be reminded of this particular picture. I know that 'mine' is not one of my regular pegs, so it must represent 12.00, not 2.00 o'clock. 'Toes' (10), being the last part of the association, represents the minutes; so I know that my swimming date is for Wednesday at 12.10.

These are the ideas that I use; but again let me stress that what is best for me is not necessarily best for you. This must be left to your own discretion; which I'm sure you will use, once you understand the basic principles involved.

You might be wondering about one little thing at this point, and that is, 'How do I differentiate between, say, 7.00 a.m. and 7.00 p.m.?' Well, that is a good theoretical question, but if you stop to think for a moment, you will realize that there can hardly be any conflict if you use this system for practical purposes. The appointments that you make for the evening are usually so vastly different from those made for the morning, that they couldn't possibly become confused. You will certainly know, for example, whether you usually see your dentist in the morning or in the evening. You also would know that your dinner date is for 7.00 p.m. and not 7.00 a.m. And, if you had an appointment to meet a friend for lunch in front of the Public Library, and got there at 1.00 a.m., you'd be awfully hungry by the time you had lunch.

So you see, there's really no problem there. Of course, if you had to, you could put a word into your ridiculous association to tell you whether it was a.m. or p.m. You could use '*aim*' for a.m. and '*poem*' for p.m., or any other words that use those letters. You might even use white and black; get black into your mental picture to stand for p.m., and white for a.m. But, believe me, all this is hardly necessary; I only mention it to show that you can remember *anything* with the use of a conscious association.

Now you can discard your note and memo pads, if you *USE* the systems explained in this chapter. Remember, only if you use it, will it help you. Here are the bare bones of the system:

When you make an appointment, transpose the day and hour (and/or minutes) to peg words.

Associate the appointment itself to these peg words.

When you rise on the morning of each day (or, if you like, the evening before) go over all your pegs for that day.

When you come to a peg that has been used in an association, you'll know it – this will remind you of what you have to do at that particular hour.

As the day goes on, you might make it a habit to check your peg words for the day, periodically. This is in case one appointment has slipped your mind, even though you were reminded of it in the morning.

In the next chapter I will show you how to remember important dates throughout the year, such as anniversaries, birthdays, etc., but for the time being, you should never forget any weekly appointments if you follow these rules.

The information you've been taught here can be practised, or used as a memory stunt in the following manner:

Have a friend call out certain errands for different hours of different days of the week. They needn't be called in order, since appointments are never made in any particular order, anyway. Have him write these down as he calls them off to you. After he has called about twenty of them, simply go over your peg words for Monday (toes, tot, tin, tomb, etc.) and call back all the Monday appointments. Do the same for each day of the entire week. Or he can give you the time of day, and the day, and you give him the errand, and so on.

Then give your friend a half-hour to remember the same list. The odds are he will fail miserably!

24 It pays to remember anniversaries, birthdays and other important dates

'Does your husband forget your anniversaries?'
'Never. I remind him of it in June, and again in January; and I always get *two* presents!'

If a man's memory is so poor that he can be led to believe that he has an anniversary every six months – then he deserves to have to buy two presents.

Seriously though, the Peg system can be applied to remembering not only important anniversaries, but also important dates in history. It is also helpful for memorizing addresses, prices or pattern numbers.

As far as dates are concerned, if you want to remember people's anniversaries or birthdays, just associate the people, or substitute words for their names, to the date, in this way: Suppose Mr Gordon's birthday is April 3rd. If you associate Mr Gordon, or the word 'garden', to 'ram', you would remember it. 'Ram' represents 43, and Mr Gordon's birthday falls in the 4th month, on the 3rd day!

Of course every date will not be able to be transposed into a basic peg word. You can do that only with those that fall within the first nine months, and for the first nine days of those months. All other dates will be a three-digit number, so a different idea must be used. I could tell you to make up a word which would represent the three-digit number, and I *will* tell you to do that in most cases. But, if done all the time, it may confuse you.

If the word in your association was 'tighten' (112), how would you know whether it meant the first month, 12th day, or the 11th month, 2nd day? You wouldn't, and your birthday card would be a bit late if you sent it on November 2nd to someone whose birthday is January 12th.

It would be late, or about two months too early.

So you must have a definite distinction to avoid this. I would suggest that the easiest way to do it is to use one word for the three digits, only for the first nine months. For October, November and December, use two words; your peg word to represent the month, and another word to represent the day. If you feel that you wouldn't know which word came first, then always use a word that is *not* a basic peg word for your day. That way you'll know that the regular peg always represents the month.

Actually this isn't necessary if you're going to use one word to represent the month and day for the first nine months. If you do, you will *know* that wherever you have two words in your association, the one that denotes two digits must represent the month, and the other the day.

If you have two words in your association, both of which denote two digits, then naturally the one over twelve would have to stand for the day. Only in the few cases where the day is either the 10th, 11th or 12th in the 10th, 11th or 12th month will you have to use the ideas suggested in the chapter on telephone numbers. You would have to use a 'logical illogical' picture to know which word comes first, or always use the basic peg word for the month, and make up a word that fits phonetically, but is *not* a regular peg word, for the day.

If, as in school work, it is necessary for you to remember the year as well as the month and day – simply get a word to represent the year into your association. For instance, although most people know the date of the signing of the American Declaration of Independence, I can use that as an example. If you associated the Declaration, or a substitute word, to 'car cash', you would know that it was signed on July 4th (7-4 – car) in the year 1776 (76 – cash). It is almost never necessary to bother with the first two digits of the year, because you would usually know the century in which an event occurred. If not, get a word for those digits into your picture, too.

School students usually have to remember only the year

of an historical event. This is easy, because all you need in your association, besides the event itself, is one word to represent the year. Napoleon was crowned emperor in the year 1804. If you made a ridiculous picture of Napoleon being crowned, and the crown hurting his head, or making it *sore* (04), you would remember it.

The Chicago fire was in 1871; just associate fire to 'cot' (71). If you made a ridiculous picture of a giant ocean liner sinking because it is made of 'tin', you would remember that the *Titanic* went down in 1912.

Sometimes it is necessary to remember the year of birth and the year of the death of important people. Just as an

example, if you made an association of a *stevedore* dressed as a *lass*, fighting a *bear* – you would recall that Robert Louis Stevenson (stevedore) was born in 1850 (lass) and died in 1894 (bear).

Now you won't be like the little boy who, when asked how he was doing in school, complained that the teacher expected him to know about things that happened before he was born!

Talking about school work, in geography it is often important to know the products that a country exports. So, why not use the Link method to remember them. Also, if you want to remember the general outline of the map of any country or state, you can always use the idea that is usually used to remember the shape of Italy.

Italy is shaped like a boot, which makes it easy to recall. If you look at the map outline of any country, with a little imagination you can make it look like something that can be pictured. Just associate that to the name of the country, and you'll always have a general idea of its shape.

Now, if you fellows want to be able to throw away those little black books full of addresses, you can. Just remember the addresses of the young ladies by using associations. The same methods apply to this. Simply transpose all the numbers into sounds, the sounds into words, and associate the words to the person living at that address. If you made a picture in your mind of yourself flying a *rope*, and *land*ing it on a *carpet* (landed rope) – it would help in remembering that Mr Karpel lives at 5211 (landed) 49th Street (rope).

The same ideas, of course, apply to pattern numbers and prices. If you happen to work in the clothing line, and wish to remember the pattern numbers of, say, dresses – associate the number to an outstanding feature of the dress. If pattern 351 is a dress with a back panel, you might 'see' that panel melting; melt – 351. The dress with puffed sleeves is pattern 3140; associate '*mattress*' to the puffed sleeves, etc.

The prices of the dresses can be included in the same association. I'm giving you only one or two examples for each idea, because it is always best for you to use your own imagination. It is entirely up to you as to which method you will use for remembering dates and how you will associate pattern numbers and prices, etc. The ideas, however, can be applied in *any* business.

Prices can be memorized just as anything else that has to do with numbers. Just associate the price to the item. To avoid confusion, you might decide always to use the basic peg words for pounds, and any other word that fits phonetically, for shillings. The same methods have to be used here as for telephone numbers and dates. You can use one word to represent three or four digits because you'll know if an item is priced in the hundreds of pounds, or not.

In America if you had associated 'maple' with book, you'd know that the price of the book is probably $3.95, and not $395.00. On the other hand, if you had associated 'maple' to television set, it would be $395.00, not $3.95, or I would buy a couple of dozen.

Well, there you are. After this you should never forget any dates, prices, pattern numbers, addresses, and so on. I must repeat that it might seem easier, at first, to write down this type of information, but after a while you will be able to associate faster than you can write.

Most important, don't worry about cluttering your mind with all these associations. Again, I want to remind you that once you have memorized the information through associations – and you *use* this particular information, well, you've etched it into your mind. The associations have served their purpose and you can forget about them.

25 Memory demonstrations

A few theatrical agents were gathered together at a carnival, to see an act that everyone was raving about. As everybody watched in awed silence, Bosco the Great climbed up a ladder to a tiny pedestal, four hundred feet in the air.

On the pedestal he took a deep breath, and then started to pump his arms to and fro. The drums rolled until they reached a noisy crescendo and, at this precise second, Bosco the Great actually left the pedestal and *flew*!

His arms pumping madly, he flew around the entire arena, up and down, back and forth.

Just then one of the agents turned to another and asked, 'Is that all he does, bird imitations?'!

I suppose that some of you are wondering why I am teaching, or have taught, all the memory feats in this book. You think that since I am a performer, and my performance *does* consist of memory stunts – I am creating competition for myself. Well, perhaps I am, but it doesn't bother me too much. I know that if any of you do want to perform in front of an audience, you will have the ingenuity to put together your own stunts and plan your own routine. And, most important, you will realize that you have to sell *yourself*, not your memory feats.

Most of the people in show business are aware of the fact that it's not what you do that makes you a good entertainer, but the *way* that you do it. The specialities that performers do are simply means to an end. Whether you tell jokes, dance, sing, do memory feats, acrobatics or bird imitations is unimportant, as long as you *entertain* your audience.

Although my main reason for teaching you the memory stunts is that the ideas used in them can be applied for practical purposes in many ways, I also feel that the best way to learn the systems is to give you an incentive by giving you something with which to show off for your friends. So, if you want to use the stunts to entertain at your lodge meeting or church affairs, feel free to do so. However, be sure that you know them well enough so that you do credit to yourself *and* my system.

There are unscrupulous characters in show business as well as in other fields, who would do anything they feel will further their careers. There is one 'culprit' who steals a new act every year or so. Last year, he did me the 'honour' of stealing my entire act, leaving out only the difficult demonstrations.

People who 'steal' material are common in show business, but to take someone's entire act is almost unheard of. However, this fellow did it, but what annoys me is not so much that he is doing my act, but that he does not do it well. This is to be expected because if he was a good entertainer he would never have to resort to using an act or idea that someone else has already built up.

No, I don't mind creating competition for myself by exposing these memory feats – as long as the competition is good. As a matter of fact, the rest of this chapter consists of stunts that I have used, and some that I still use occasionally.

One of the stunts you can use is remembering objects and initials. First have your friends call any object and any two initials. Do this with as many as you feel you can handle. Then you have the audience call any object and you give them the initials, or vice versa.

This stunt is not only impressive, but easy to do. Just make up a word that starts with the first initial and ends with the last, and associate that word to the object called.

For example: if the initials are R. T., and the object is 'chandelier', you might associate *rat* to chandelier. The initials B. D. and bottle – associate *bed* to bottle. The initials P. S. and fan – associate *puss* to fan, etc.

Here is another example of how the systems can be twisted

and manipulated – you can do the 'missing card' stunt with *numbers* if you want to. Have someone number a sheet of paper from 1 to 52, or up to any number you like. Have them call numbers haphazardly and cross out the numbers as they call them. They can stop calling them any time they like, and you can tell them which numbers are *not* crossed out!

Do exactly as you do for the 'missing cards'. Just mutilate the peg words which represent the numbers called. Then go over your words mentally from 'tie' to the peg word of the last number listed on the paper. When you come to one that is *not* mutilated, that is one of the 'missing' numbers.

One very impressive card demonstration is the 'hidden card' feat. This is most effective when you are working for a group of at least fifty-two people. (For less people, use less cards.) Hand the pack to the audience and let everyone take one card. Now, have each person call the name of his card and also give you a hiding-place for it.

What you do is associate the card word for the card called to the hiding-place. If someone called the Jack of Spades hidden in a typewriter, you would perhaps see yourself shovelling typewriters (with a *spade*).

After all the cards have been 'hidden', you can hear the name of a card and immediately give the hiding-place. Or, you are given the hiding-place, and you name the card hidden there!

Do you want to impress your friends with your ability to remember numbers? Well, if you've learned another peg list up to 16 or 20, as I've taught you, you can do this:

Have your challenger number a piece of paper from 1 to 16 or 20. Then have him call any of these numbers and write a two-digit number alongside. When all the numbers have been called, you can go from one to the end telling him the two-digit numbers – or, have him call any two-digit number and you tell him what number it is at, or vice versa.

Just use your other list to remember the sequence, and use your basic pegs for the two-digit numbers, i.e. 3 is called, and the two-digit number to remember is 34. Well, if you're using the alphabet list, you would associate 'sea' (3) to 'mower' (34). Then 14 is called and the number to remember is 89 – associate 'hen' (14) to 'fob' (89).

If you feel confident, you can have your friends call an object *and* a two-digit number for each number listed. You can memorize both, by making one ridiculous picture for all three. The number called could be 9, the object is a toaster, and the two-digit number is 24. Any combination of associations is possible here; you could see Nero (24) popping out of a toaster, playing on an eye (9) instead of a fiddle! I have been using the alphabet list idea in these examples. Of course you could use the other idea wherein the pegs look like the numbers they represent. In that case, 9 would be 'tape measure', 3 would be 'clover', 14 would be 'farm', etc.

Any one of the systems in this book can be used for a stunt of some sort, just as the ideas for all the stunts can be used for practical purposes in some way. If you want to apply substitute words to a stunt you can memorize names and playing cards, names and objects, and so on. You can utilize the system for remembering long digit numbers, by having people call their names *and* the serial number on a pound note, or their car number. Then you should be able to give the number when you hear the name, and give the name if you hear the number. To do this you simply make up a substitute word for the name, if necessary; associate that to the peg word for the first two digits of the number, and make a link to the end of the number.

Although the following is not actually a stunt, the idea grew from the initial and object feat that I mentioned earlier. The Morse code is a very difficult thing to remember because it is almost completely abstract and intangible. The dots and dashes are meaningless and cannot be pictured.

I don't suppose that too many of you will ever find it necessary to have to remember the Morse code. However, I do want you to see that there is no limit to what you can do with conscious associations, and the knowledge that anything meaningless is easy to remember if it is made meaningful. Your only limitation is your own imagination.

Since dots and dashes have no meaning I decided to give
them meaning by making the letter R stand for dot, and the
letter T or D represent the dash. With this in mind, you can
make up a word or phrase for each letter, which can be
pictured and that will tell you the code signal for that letter.
Look at this list:

A	.—	rat	N	—.	tier
B	—...	terror	O	———	touted
C	—.—.	torture	P	.——.	rotator
D	—..	tearer	Q	——.—	tethered
E	.	air	R	.—.	writer
F	..—.	rear tyre	S	...	roarer
G	——.	tighter	T	—	toe
H	....	rarer rye	U	..—	rarity
I	..	rower	V	...—	re-arrest
J	.———	ratted	W	.——	retied
K	—.—	trout	X	—..—	turret
L	.—..	retire her	Y	—.——	treated
M	——	toad	Z	——..	teeterer

All that remains to be done is to associate the word to the
letter itself, so that one will remind you of the other. You
could use the peg words that sound like the letters –
associate ape to rat, bean to terror, sea to torture, dean to
tearer, eel to air, effort to rear tyre, and so on to zebra
to teeterer.

Or you could use the adjective idea by associating an
adjective that begins with the proper letter to the word –
awful rat, big terror, crazy torture, dreamy tearer,
excellent air, flat tyre, and so on to zigzag teeterer. If you
know the position of all the letters, then you could just use
your regular peg words, by associating them to the signal
word.

The way you associate them is up to you. The idea is that
now the dots and dashes are no longer unintelligible. It
shouldn't take you more than half an hour to memorize the
Morse code with this system. Of course, this doesn't mean
that you will be a telegraphist. Speed in sending code comes

only with lots of practice and experience, but the system does make it easier at the beginning, when you have to memorize the signals.

So you see how the systems can be twisted and manipulated to help you with almost any memory problem. I've tried to teach you many stunts in this chapter and throughout the book, and I'm sure you'll be able to think of many more.

. . . And then there was this theatrical agent who was watching an act with a friend. The act was on a high wire, hundreds of feet above the ground. There was no net to catch him if he fell.

He balanced a golf ball on the wire, and balanced a chair, upside down, on the golf ball. He then proceeded to stand on his head on one of the upturned chair legs. In this precarious position, he began to play a violin with his *feet*!

The theatrical agent turned to his associate and sneered, 'Aah, a Jascha Heifetz he'll never be!'

26 Use the systems

A violin virtuoso living in America truly believed that he could play so well that he could actually charm a savage beast. Despite the warnings and pleas of his friends, he decided he would go to darkest Africa, unarmed, with only his violin.

He stood in a clearing in the dense jungle and began to play.

An elephant received his scent and came charging towards him; but, when he came within hearing distance, he sat down to listen to the beautiful music.

A panther sprang from a tree with fangs bared, but also succumbed to the music. Soon a lion appeared to join the others. Before long, many wild animals were seated near the virtuoso; he played on, unharmed.

Just then a leopard leaped from a nearby tree, on to the violinist, and devoured him! As he stood licking his chops the other animals approached, and asked, 'Why did you do that? The man was playing such lovely music!'

The leopard, cupping his ear, said, 'Eh, what did you say?'

So you see, no matter how beautiful music is, unfortunately, if you can't hear it, it doesn't mean a thing. Similarly, no matter how useful and helpful the systems in this book are, they won't do you a bit of good if you don't *use* them.

I do hope that most of you have given some time and thought to them. If you have, you should be pleased with the progress you've made. The flexibility of the systems, I believe, is their greatest asset. I, personally, have yet to come across anything, pertaining to memory, to which the systems were not applicable.

Take the time necessary to learn how to make conscious associations, and once you've mastered it, it will take care of itself. Every once in a while you may come across some

piece of information that you want to remember, that is
made to order for an association. If an American wanted to
remember that a certain item sold for $17.76, he could, of
course, use peg words as has been shown. However, you
have all heard of the 'Spirit of '76'. That phrase will create a
picture for most of us of the famous portrayal of the
'Spirit of '76'; a man with a drum, a man with a fife, and
the third holding the American flag. If you were to associate
the item in question with this picture you would recall that
$17.76 was the price.

The Japanese volcano, Fujiyama, is 12,365 feet high.
Again, you could use peg words to remember this, or you
could associate Fujiyama to 'calendar'. The reason for
'calendar' is that the number of feet is the amount of
months in a year (12), and the amount of days in a year
(365). You would associate calendar either to volcano, or a
substitute word for Fujiyama.

I'm not suggesting that you do this with all numbers; the
Peg system is the only infallible one. However, looking for
numbers that fall into this category is good for your
imagination and observation, and it helps create an *interest*
in numbers.

In an early chapter I told you that you could remember
the names of the Dionne quintuplets by remembering the
word 'macey'. Now you know that in order to remember the
word, you would have to associate the quins *to* 'macey'.
You might 'see' Macy's Department Store in New York
completely packed with quins, etc. If you want to know the
names of the four living quins, drop the odd e, for Emilie,
and you'll remember, *M*arie, *A*nnette, *C*ecile and *Y*vonne.

This idea would aid you in recalling the names of the five
Great Lakes. If you made a picture in your mind of a lot of
'homes' on a great lake you would always remember that
the Lakes are Lake *H*uron, *O*ntario, *M*ichigan, *E*rie and
*S*uperior!

If you've learned to make up substitute words quickly and
easily this will become your greatest move towards a better

memory. Actually, I should say substitute thoughts or pictures; you know by now that it is the picture created in your mind that's important, not the word itself.

Did you know that the capital of New Mexico is Santa Fe? Well, make a picture of *Santa* Claus wearing a *Mexican* sombrero, and you'll probably never forget it. If you 'see' yourself throwing *little rocks* at an *ark*, you'll have no trouble recalling that Little Rock is the capital city of *Ark*ansas. Do you know a girl whose name is Helen or Helena? Picture her climbing a *mount*ain, to help you remember that Helena is the capital of Montana. If you picture *boys* eating raw potatoes, you'll remember that *Boise* is the capital of Idaho (Idaho potatoes). Of course, you could picture *Ida hoe*ing *boys*, and get the same result.

You understand, I'm sure, that it would have been impossible for me to give direct examples of how my systems are applicable to all businesses. Be assured that they *are* applicable to just about anything where memory is involved. Your own particular problem may require a certain twist or change of one of the systems, but *you* would know that better than I.

Nowadays, most of us are diet conscious, and I've noticed

people carrying around little calorie counters to tell them what not to eat. Well, this is fine, but you could use the Peg system to help you memorize the amount of calories contained in the foods you usually eat. If you made a ridiculous picture between a fried egg and 'disease', you'd know that a fried egg contained 100 calories. Did you know that one tablespoon of mayonnaise contained 92 calories? Well, if you associate it to 'bone', you won't forget it. If you keep gaining weight, and you drink lots of draught beer, you ought to associate 'tackle' to the beer, and you'll remember that an 8-ounce glass contains 175 calories.

If any of you still feel that it is too much trouble to use my methods, let me repeat that I call this the 'lazy man's' way of remembering. It is the so-called 'natural' or rote method of memory that is difficult. Not only is it difficult, but not as efficient, not as retentive, not as rewarding, and not as much fun. Most important, my methods are unlimited. At the risk of seeming repetitious – 'you are limited only by your own imagination'.

I just used the word 'repetitious', which reminded *me* to mention the fact that many students have trouble remembering that this word is spelled with an e, not an i. If you would print the word on a piece of paper, making e extra large, make it stand out (rep*E*titious) and look at it for a while, you won't misspell it again. If you want to catch your friends, ask them to spell the word 'liquefy'. I think nine out of ten people will put an i before the f, instead of an e. Print the word like this: liqu *E* fy; look at it and concentrate on it for a moment, and the chances are you'll spell it correctly from now on. Try this with any word that you are not sure of, and you'll certainly improve your spelling.

Many of the ideas that were taught to you were taught as memory feats. I've done this for a variety of reasons. First, I believe that it makes it much easier to learn, because you can actually see your goal. I've seen too many people start to try to learn something, and then soon give it up because they couldn't see the use or benefit of it right in front of their eyes. Seeing the goal gives you an added incentive to learn. The fact that you can use the feats to entertain your friends is an extra added incentive.

When you can do or understand the stunts you've grasped the idea, and that's all I care about. Once you've got the idea you will be able to apply it when you need it. This is where you must put your imagination to work. Any memory problem that may present itself *can* be solved by using one or more of the methods and systems, whether they were taught to you in the form of a memory demonstration or otherwise.

My purpose in writing this book has been to give you the basis and groundwork of a trained memory. The systems are more far-reaching and more applicable than the space allowed me could possibly show. I do hope, however, that I have given you an inkling of what can be done with my systems. The rest is up to you!

Alvin Toffler
Future Shock 95p

Future shock is the disease of change. Its symptoms are already here ... *Future Shock* tells what happens to people overwhelmed by too rapid change ... And looks at the human side of tomorrow.

Brilliantly disturbing, the book analyses the new and dangerous society now emerging, and shows how to come to terms with the future.

'An important book reaching some startling conclusions' BBC

'If this book is neglected we shall all be very foolish' C. P. SNOW

Martin Pawley
The Private Future 60p

Is man increasingly a prisoner of his dreams? Self — not community — has become all-important; cars are machines for 'getting away from it all'; sport is for watching on TV; sexual fantasies bring orgasm without conception; films present a violent, erotic, anti-social image ... Is Western society facing Doomsday?

With all the force of *Future Shock* — 'A chilling analysis of contemporary social trends ... predicts a nightmare future' EVENING NEWS

Robert H. Thouless
Straight and Crooked Thinking 50p

The ideal of straight thinking must be the application of the scientific habit of thought to all your practical problems. This book deals with those situations where cold, unemotional thinking is needed. In addition the author, an eminent psychologist, tells you how to protect yourself from other people's crooked thinking, and the intellectual exploitation attempted by unscrupulous public speakers. He enumerates thirty-eight Dishonest Tricks commonly used in argument and suggests methods of overcoming them.

Dr Jack Birnbaum
How to Stop Hating and Start Loving 70p

Based on the principles of Transactional Analysis and Gestalt Therapy, Dr Birnbaum's excellent book shows how anger — expressed or suppressed, in the right way and at the right time — can become therapeutic: you are free again to feel affection and joy. You can stop hating and start loving!

Thomas A. Harris MD
I'm OK – You're OK 80p

A practical guide to Transactional Analysis. This phenomenal breakthrough in psychotherapy has proved a turning point for thousands of Americans.

An important new method of helping people, Transactional Analysis brings a refreshingly practical approach to the problems we all encounter in day-to-day relationships with ourselves and other people. In sensible, non-clinical language Thomas Harris tells how to gain control of your life and be responsible for your future — *no matter what has happened in the past*.

Dr Richard Mackarness
Not All in the Mind 60p

In this new and vitally important book, Dr Richard Mackarness, doctor and psychiatrist, shows how millions may be made ill, physically and mentally, by common foods such as milk, eggs, coffee and white flour.

He relates case after case from his clinical practice where patients with chronic ailments resistant to other methods of treatment were cured by identifying and eliminating foods to which they had developed unsuspected allergy. The history and mechanics of this unique approach to ordinary though disabling complaints are given in fascinating detail.

Dr Mackarness also describes how you and your doctor can identify and cure your allergy by a simple method without drugs — before it is too late.

Peter Blythe
Stress – The Modern Sickness 60p

Why is stress an ever-increasing problem? How does the mind convert stress into physical illness? When can stress lead to a broken marriage? Is being over-weight a stress symptom?

These and many other vital questions are discussed by Peter Blythe, a practising psychotherapist and consultant hypnotist, who examines every aspect of normal living and shows where the build-up of anxiety-stress-tension plays a determining part in a variety of illnesses.

Dr Joan Gomez
How Not to Die Young 70p

Are you living dangerously?

With the aid of two hundred and forty practical, multi-choice questions, Dr Gomez indicates the many different actions and dangerous habits which could do your health irrevocable harm, and shows how unnecessary deaths can be avoided.

Mildred Newman and Bernard Berkowitz
How to be Your Own Best Friend 35p

This remarkable book, written with warmth, understanding and wisdom, provides simple guidelines to help you become the person it is in you to be.

'There is no pill made that is as simple, effective and fast-working ... positively inspirational' NEIL SIMON

You can buy these and other Pan books from booksellers and newsagents; or direct from the following address:
Pan Books, Cavaye Place, London SW10 9PG
Send purchase price plus 15p for the first book and 5p for each additional book, to allow for postage and packing
Prices quoted are applicable in UK
While every effort is made to keep prices low, it is sometimes necessary to increase prices at short notice. Pan Books reserve the right to show on covers new retail prices which may differ from those advertised in the text or elsewhere